Horus Templar

and the

Case of the Iniquitous Inquisitor

E.L. WARD

Horus Templar and the Case of the Iniquitous Inquisitor is a work of fiction. Names, characters, places, and incidents either are the product of the author's imagination or are used fictitiously. Any resemblance to actual persons, living or dead, events, or locales is entirely coincidental.

ISBN: 978-1-7370436-1-4

Table of Contents

"Run from your shame. Flee utterly from it. You deserve to see: there is no distance great enough."

- Magormissahr, *Referendums on the World, Vol. 971*

Chapter 1

It began with a rather pitiful cry for help.

Captain Alexei had already grown long of chin and dry of mouth that morning – a broad day, it was, with every indication of broadening ever on. He found himself in the midst of a heavy chore. Freshly-minted, punitive laws had just been passed down from the Czarina, and the entire SAPD was out in force, trying their best to explain new regulations to a thoroughly bewildered populace. With the vast throngs of people living in the city of St. Argonsburg, this would have been work enough. That the unsuspecting policemen did not understand the new laws *themselves* certainly did not help...

Thus it was that, as the faint echo of, "HELP! POLICE!" met the Captain's ear, he was only too relieved to excuse himself from a crowd abuzz with overlapping questions and charge headlong into potential disaster. His strides carried him quickly through the alleys between the little shops and depots that dotted the coastal market, until he came to the place he supposed the shout had originated...

Freezing in his tracks, the sight that met his eyes allayed all doubt. Just before him there was a small ticket booth, whose clerk stood quaking – his face drawn back in deathly horror. And it was no wonder why. On the counter... mere *inches* in front of the clerk... was a huge pile of money!

"What happened here, Sir?" Alexei asked – sternly, as if to shake the man from a paralysis.

"H-he..." the clerk faltered, "...he tried to *pay* me!"

Alexei dismissed the question of 'who' at once – there wasn't time for it. Truly, a great crime had been committed here... and the guilty could *not* be permitted to escape! "Which way did he *go*?"

"Th-that way!" the clerk said, shaky finger extended.

Alexei held fast his hat as he sprung hot on the trail, quickly gaining speed. Even once he reached full-clip, he found he didn't grow unsure of himself while he raced along the paths at the Harbor's edge. This came as some surprise. A single market district down here boasted far more buildings and people than the entirety of his hometown. It had all seemed so daunting at first... but already he could almost *feel* his way around the vast city...

He felt it well enough, in fact, that after only a few buildings, he caught a fleeting glimpse of the perpetrator – a veiled and cloaked shadow, the man looked – darting down a parallel path. Alexei was at once a bit mystified. The crime committed had not even *been* a crime the day before, and already this perp was dressing the part of a ghastly menace to society. He had to shake down some haunting memories, as they bit at his heels. For a cop from little-old Podunkville, Alexei was an unlikely veteran of at least one exceedingly dark caper already... far darker than anything he cared to let on about... or even remember, if it could be helped. But at the sight of the suspect, he had the presence of mind to blow his police whistle, even as he privately pled with the Creators that he wasn't just about to get mixed up in anything like *that* again...

Soon, he heard the whistles of fellow officers sound over buildings all around. Other figures in royal blue coats and bobbies were leaping to the chase from adjoining alleys. Some approached him, only to be silently redirected with a quick hand-signal from their captain. Alexei's adrenaline began to kick-in as he spurned himself onward, feeling a strange new confidence. Neither the urban life nor the onus of command made him doubt a single stride...

Just one building behind a major crossroads, he caught another flash of movement out of the corner of his spectacles. The shadowy suspect had hung a right. Alexei blew another signal on his whistle as he rounded the bend. Here, in this wider lane, he got his first good look at the criminal... albeit while his field of vision was jostling wildly with each long, urgent step. It was a sight that quite nearly staggered him. The hood, the cloak... it was all affectingly familiar... something not just he, but *anyone* would recognize. But this made no sense. The build, size, and mechanics of the suspect did not lie... Alexei knew on an instinctual level he was chasing a fellow *Human*. And anyway, anyone so dressed should not be fleeing from the cops... much less have a heap of cash to leave behind...

Before he could even begin to puzzle it over, the suspect veered off the main lane. In a grand sort of convergence, Alexei was finally arrested in his tracks as someone *else* trudged into the road in front of him...

"Ah, there you are," grumbled a winded old man: none other than the Deputy Constable, Stenya Miloje. He flung his hands to his knees as he gasped for much-needed air. "What is all the dratted excitement about, Captain?"

"A flagrant breach of the new laws, Sir," Alexei declared, saluting his boss. "We are in pursuit of the suspect."

Miloje waved him on by. "Well, then, as you were! Your legs will serve far better than mine!"

Alexei nodded and leapt back to the chase, feeling the more encouraged that his superior entrusted this task to him... even if his poor physical condition probably left him little choice. Even so, he knew he'd lost precious moments and was now certainly quite far behind. His only hope to close the gap was to try to deduce where the perp was fleeing before he got there... to put himself in the criminal mind, so to speak. Grizzled city cops were supposed to be able to do stuff like that...

He thought back to the scene of the crime... a ticket booth... a place for travelers to purchase fare on a ship. Whoever – and *whatever* – this criminal was, he must be eminently motivated to skip the country... if the amount of money he'd used to try to force a ticket sale was any indication. The route of his flight reinforced this... the right turn would have directed him back toward the coast...

This gave Alexei the advantage he needed. Rather than stalk the suspect through a series of back-alleys – which his fellows were doing an adequate job of anyway – he decided to stay on the lane and keep making full bore for the docks...

* * *

It wasn't long before Alexei found himself hunkered behind a trifecta of wooden shipping barrels, conveniently left lined up along a dock that berthed two passenger ships on each side. There were, admittedly, dozens of docks like this within a mile's stretch of the Great Harbor, but this was the one most in line with the suspect's last known flight path, so there was no finer dock to gamble on...

Thoroughly concealed, he set to loading his police sidearm – a new pistol he had far from mastered. He made his own stride longer than the suspect's – as it was longer than most Humans', anyway – and he trusted his fellow officers to make his approach a difficult and cautious one... but even so, Alexei sensed he had little time to prepare...

Sure enough, he heard rapid footfalls beating on the boardwalk within moments of opening the tumbler. He scarcely had time to fumble one bullet into the gun and the footfalls were already even with him. He threw himself up with his sidearm outstretched. "Stop! In the name of the Law!" he called...

The flurried feet of the suspect didn't skip a beat.

Alexei cringed. Whatever he'd seen and done before – even having been put up to a 'battle to the death' once – he'd never *shot* someone... never taken a life himself. He didn't want to. But his sworn duty demanded he use every means to arrest the perpetrator... and he had a clear shot. He'd have it only a step or two longer...

BANG

The suspect managed several more steps – odd, unnatural, his upper body flailing just to try to keep him moving – before he finally collapsed. Alexei rushed to the scene, heedless of any danger to himself, only hoping that the criminal could survive whatever wound he'd just inflicted... even if it was only to later face the state executioner. Reaching the form of the man – still clawing on the ground as if to crawl aboard a ship – he found the wound easily enough. It was high and wide... somewhere between the shoulder and the back... a place Alexei thanked the Creators he was pretty sure had no vital organs. But there was blood... and a man could only lose so much of that. It didn't help, him thrashing around the way he was. The situation was still critical...

Alexei stood aghast for a few moments as he absently detected the sound of more running on the docks. A few police sergeants soon joined him, fanned around the prone frame of their quarry.

"You got him, Captain," Sergeant Huxley said.

"Yes, I'm afraid so," Alexei agreed, paying little mind. He needed to stop the man still trying to move...

"I say Sir," he called to the suspect, kneeling down and working to physically restrain him. "Give it up! You've been had. There is no sense in further resistance..."

Practically wrestling the cloaked perpetrator, Alexei's anger quickly spiked. His every effort to warn him and to stop him for his own good had so far gone ignored. He needed to get the man's attention. He went to throw him over on his back...

"I say now..." he began, but his words stopped up as he saw the man's face for the first time. Or... what *would* have been his face. Yes, there was no denying Alexei's earlier recognition of the hood and cloak now. For in addition to these standardized features, the suspect wore a *mask*... a smooth, reflective thing, whose visor could not be made out from the rest

of the practically featureless inverted-teardrop-shape of his headdress. Even if the clothing had been a mere facsimile, there was no mistaking such a mask...

"Dianodes," Sergeant Tarkinov cursed under his breath. "He's... he's a... I mean, you... you shot..."

"Creators save me, but I did," Alexei interjected, his own voice sounding foreign to him as it echoed weakly across his private ocean of bewilderment. "I shot an Inquisitor."

Chapter 2

"Objection!" Horus called as he stood.

"Carried," Judge Felix nodded. He raised his chin as he looked over at the prosecution, though she took no notice. "Your witness must refrain from volunteering conclusions."

"Of course, your Honor," Blucille Cordon said, sounding passably apologetic, even if her eyes never left her overloaded clipboard. "Now, Ms. Djerkovic..."

"*Mrs.*, if you please, Deary," the kindly old lady corrected her. "My Richard is gone, but not forgotten."

"My apologies, Ma'am," Cordon replied, snatching up the clipboard and making a few quick, violent scratches. Then she also stood... perhaps as a token effort to seem more engaged in the moment. "Mrs. Djerkovic, this is a crucial point. The court requires that you report the results of your financial audit... sans any color commentary."

"Why certainly," Vesta Djerkovic beamed. Horus would have found her chipper manner amusing, if he weren't professionally cautious of eager witnesses. "My audit did not reveal any mistakes that would account for the defendant's deficit. The number of transactions, as well as the value of each, matched the bank records. How ever Mr. Boris managed to make off with his own company's money, he must've been mighty clever about it."

Horus stood again. "Objection."

Judge Felix sighed. "Well, never mind. We have the report. The court recorder will strike that last statement and we will proceed." He furrowed a brow at Horus. "That is, unless the defense is quite insistent."

Horus quickly thought better of it. "Objection withdrawn."

As Horus sat back down, his client caught him in a sidebar. "Say, whose side are you on?" Boris whispered.

Horus leaned over, keeping an ear pointed at the proceedings. "Whatever I do, I can't delay her report forever... much less change the findings. The key to your defense doesn't lie in concealing the obvious facts, but in unearthing the conspicuously absent ones. We'll get to the bottom of your missing money yet."

"Alright," Boris groaned. "Just don't go withdrawing any more objections on me. It's enough to make a guy nervous."

Horus just nodded. His latest client was a bit of an abrasive fellow, all things considered – an owner of a profitable vineyard that had been brought to court over a relatively minor discrepancy in their financial records. It was far from the most serious crime in the country... generally punishable on a first offense with only heavy fines. Profitable businesses, after all, should be disciplined and allowed to continue on, lest significant revenue be lost needlessly...

Once Cordon had Mrs. Djerkovic report the total missing revenue – 315 pence and 85 shillings – she sat back down. "I am finished with this witness," she declared, pen already blazing new trails on her clipboard.

"Cross examine," Felix instructed Horus.

Horus rose, locking eyes with the elderly Human woman for a goodly interval. She had a pleasant smile that, even as he concentrated his gaze, seemed impenetrable. Yes, no matter how he tried, he couldn't get an exact fix on her. She was either the ultimate doting old lady, or a psychopath... or both. But at least that narrowed it down...

"Your Honor," Horus said at length, not breaking his stare right away. "The defense has no wish to examine the witness at this time. Rather, we request leave of the court to conduct our own audit." Even at this, there was no crack in Mrs. Djerkovic's front...

The courtroom was silent again for a moment. "Is there no objection from the prosecution?"

"None, your Honor," Cordon answered. "Mr. Templar will only point out the precedent in Hientz vs. Heckman's."

Felix shook his head somewhat despondently. "Even so, the request of the defense will take significant time. Mrs. Djerkovic's financial credentials are sound. Is a second audit quite necessary?"

"Oh, very much so, your Honor," Horus explained. "It's either that, or for my defense I shall have to begin calling the various patrons, vendors and contractors of Vineyard 359... *every single one* of them over the last month."

Judge Felix blanched. "Court is dismissed," he said with a quick rap of his gavel. "All parties will be notified when the second audit is completed. A date and time to reconvene will be announced then."

While people began filing out, Boris let into Horus again. "A second audit!? You were just talking about uncovering *new* facts, not taking another look at old ones! What will a second audit prove?"

"Perhaps nothing," Horus shrugged, before plastering on a sage expression. "Perhaps... *everything*."

Boris just groaned and stormed away. But it was well that he did so, for just as he left, Horus was approached by the State's auditor... the very lady he needed most to talk to...

"Hello, Mrs. Djerkovic," he greeted her. "I'm glad you came over; I meant to apologize. Honestly, I'm over a barrel on this case – having another look at the books seems the only thing I can possibly do in the interest of my client. I certainly hope you won't take it as a slight to your work. I don't mean to reflect negatively on you."

"Not at all, young man," the sickly-sweet lady assured him. "It's the negative things in life that sometimes have the greatest payoff. I'm actually grateful for a second audit."

Horus' ears set. "You are?"

"Oh, yes. Let's face it, Deary... one look into my tired old eyes, and people will question whether I've still got it. A second audit to confirm my work should allay doubts for a while longer, I'd like to think."

Horus grinned and nodded. "Well, in that case, you're most welcome."

He turned to go, but she stopped him. "The fact is, Mr. Templar, I'd consider myself in your debt. You simply *must* let me know what your bill ends up being for the audit, and I'll reimburse you."

Horus searched her face... a smile on it too powerful for his truth-inducing eyes, even at close range. "That hardly seems necessary, Mrs. Djerkovic."

"Now, don't fight me on this," she insisted, holding out her checkbook. "I've spent a lifetime balancing books, and I want to come away from this feeling like you and I are square."

He hesitated.

"Don't make me ask pretty-please," she went on.

Horus finally assented. "Alright, Mrs. Djerkovic. You have my thanks."

"No, Deary." Her 'tired old eyes' glinted as she shook her head. "Thank *you*."

* * *

Minutes later, Horus ambled out of the courtroom. He had only time enough to barely register what seemed like an elevated level of hubbub in the halls of the capitol courthouse, when Blucille Cordon suddenly caught up with him...

"A moment, Templar?" she asked him.

He looked back at her mischievously. "Are you sure you want to talk now? It seems just the other day you wanted to reprimand me for trying to discuss a case outside of court..."

She shrugged disinterestedly. "Yes, and then we proceeded to talk all about it; this is nothing new. I wanted to convey the State's gratitude that you're going to take your customary hard look at those books... in fact, to encourage you to take the hardest look you can."

Horus' eyes bugged. "Well, that *is* new."

She reached into her bag and handed him a bunch of file folders. "There's something bigger going on here, Templar. It's not just Vineyard 359... ten businesses in the metropolitan area are in court right now over missing funds."

He considered that pensively. "Ten at once, you say? How exactly were all these deficits brought to the attention of the State?"

After a quick check of her pocket watch, she gestured for them to continue talking on the run. "I wish I had a better answer for that," she said, as they began shuffling further down the hall. "It started when we got word from an anonymous tipster, concerning another of the city's major vineyards, and we followed up on it. The tip held water. We've had nine more tips and counting since... and not one so far has missed."

"A *tipster*," Horus repeated. "That's just what I thought."

Cordon shot a grimace across his bow. "*Thought*? I suppose you already knew something about this larger conspiracy..."

"Maybe a little. But to have a complete list from you – and to know about the tipster – that tends to advance things."

"Well, I'm sure you'll agree it can't be a series of isolated incidents. Someone must be defrauding these companies, and the state financiers are desperate to find out who it is."

"So they can make an example of him?"

She shook her head. "So they can *hire* him."

"Ah, yes... my mistake."

"We'll do everything we can on our end," she said as they rounded a bend in the hall. "But we value your assistance. You're the brightest Public Defender we have attached to this." She paused, like she had to wind herself up to say something more. "And... in *Blackforest's* opinion... you have the allegiance of the city's best investigator."

Horus grinned. "I'll be sure to relay *Blackforest's* high praise to Art."

This time, she sneered directly at him. "Don't be *cute*. And try to keep us in the loop, if your theatrical mind can stand it. But for now, good day. I'm due in court again in ten minutes, and I need a puff." She started down a side hall to the patio before she even finished her statement...

"Good day to *you*, Ms. Cordon," Horus replied... if only to himself. As usual, she was already out of earshot...

He took a cleansing breath, washing away a feeling like a passing whirlwind that Cordon tended to stick him with. Things had gone well today in court. Moreover, he was grateful merely to have found another case so shortly after his blockbuster Mantid trial. Truth be told, he felt pretty good: sleek of fur and comfortably engaged in meaningful work. It seemed a fine moment to just sort of pause and enjoy a bit of repose. Passively taking in the immediate surroundings, he chanced to look down at his own feet. It was also a fine moment, he decided, for an overdue shoeshine...

* * *

Sometimes, unaccountably, the instincts of even the most intuitive individual fly the coup at just the inopportune moment. Between the clusters of murmuring people in the halls, the wide-eyed searching of Vlad the shoe-shiner as he plopped down into the seat, and the scent of fear swirling furiously in the air, Horus should've known something was up. But... he didn't. He sat back at ease, taking only the dimmest notice of Vlad's slow, cautious approach...

"Can... can I help you, Mr. Templar?" Vlad asked, rending his rag in his hands.

"I *hope* you can," Horus replied, almost chuckling. "My shoes are in a bad way, Vlad... dull as the day they were cut out of dinosaur-hide." He extended his little feet.

"You... *really* want me to shine your shoes?" Vlad continued. "Are you sure that's wise... you know... under the circumstances?"

Horus took his head off the rest and winced questioningly at the man. "*Wise*?" He tried to laugh it off. "I'm not sure I understand the question." He looked at his shoes again. "Maybe these *are* in even worse shape than I thought." Then, he reached for his money bag. "How about I kick in five extra shillings for this round..."

His hand was not an inch above the lip of the bag when someone reached out and stopped it. Numerous onlookers gasped at the close call. Vlad appeared nearly faint. Horus looked puzzled at the hand clasped around his wrist. Then he looked up...

"Tisk-tisk, Boss," Deborah said, shaking her head at him. "You know better than to go without checking the bulletin board, when you've been shut up in chambers all day."

He kept looking dumbfounded up into her lovely eyes, his mind perplexed, and his heart fluttering. "Some new edict against shoe-shining?" he asked at length.

"*Well...*" she said, letting go of his wrist and clasping his hand, helping him up from the seat, "...not *quite*. I think you better see this one for yourself."

Trading glances at her and the gathered crowd of gawkers, Horus found he was in no hurry to check the board. Evidently there *was* a new law of the land... and it must've been a doozy...

But, after a moment of mustering himself, he crossed the hall to the nearest posting. He quickly homed in on the latest decree, stamped with the seal of the Seven Pearls...

He read it. He read it again. He read it a *third* and *fourth* time. But he couldn't believe...

"*What in the wide Undervoid*?"

Chapter 3

"That's right... *no economy,*" Art Mallard explained, leaning against the wall of Horus' office car while the Public Defender paced the floor. "Zilch. Zippo. Not one red cent allowed to change hands anywhere."

"But how will...? Or, what will we...? How do we...?" Horus asked.

"Believe me, I've been asking the same questions all morning."

Horus stopped impatiently. "Well, out with it then, Art! What are the answers!?"

Art flicked away a thoroughly used toothpick. "I don't know. Nobody knows."

"But surely a great private eye like you would've learned *something,*" Deborah jumped in. "Do you at least have an inkling why the Czarina would outlaw her own economy?"

"That much I can explain. Remember that trade war we were in with Maenea?"

"I *do* remember," Horus answered. "But probably not as well as you do."

"Darn tootin'," Art nodded.

"Well never mind," Deborah insisted, folding her arms. "What could a silly little trade war have to do with this? It hasn't been in the papers for *months*. I thought it was over with by now..."

"Oh, it's over all right," Art laughed. "Only it didn't end the way our silly little trade wars tend to." He skipped a beat for dramatic effect. "We *lost*."

Horus blanched. "*Lost*?" He puzzled mightily for a moment. So far, Art's explanations were just leading from one impossible bit of nonsense to another. "How does one even go about losing a trade war?" he asked. "No... that question falls utterly short. How does *Jast-Madiir* go about losing a trade war? And of all places, against *Maenea*?"

Art threw up his hands. "Hey, I'm a PI, not an economist. And a good thing, too. The economists can't figure it out either. I only hope for their sakes the sight of the chopping block inspires some last-minute epiphany."

"I can't imagine," Deborah sighed. "We've never lost a trade war before, have we? Surely we haven't..."

"No, and that's exactly the point. The Czarina's furious – like next-level furious. She can't abide a lost trade war. Banning the economy is apparently her way of freezing her losses... and taking it out on the whole country in the process."

"What a disaster," Horus said absently. "How long do you suppose it'll last?"

"Well, there's nothing in the language of the edict that would suggest an end date. But me, I give it a week, tops."

Horus picked up and gave a copy of the new law another scan. "The language of the edict is lacking in all sorts of ways. The economy's illegal now... but it's also a capital crime to be caught not doing your job. How are people supposed to reconcile two laws like that?"

Art shrugged. "Some are just finding busywork... cleaning and re-cleaning. I guess a few people are giving out their goods and services pro bono... although most are too afraid to be seen doing something that *looks* economical."

"The worst of it might be the transportation situation," Deborah said. "Most of the rails and carriages are only making dry runs. People are out there scrambling to get to work on time... only to do nothing when they get there."

Horus remembered coming up to the train station with an involuntary shiver. The urbanites of St. Argonsburg had been dashing full-speed all around him on foot. He'd watched the conductors of the train swing out and dutifully call, "All aboard!" before frantically bolting the doors shut again behind themselves. He was just lucky he had the keys to his own car. Looking out through his window now, the scene had not improved. People were running everywhere, looking panicked. He shook his head. "It's like the whole country turned into a madhouse overnight."

"And at just the worst time, too," Art lamented, looking down morosely at the fingers of his right hand, curled over in his palm. "I really needed to get my nails done today."

As Horus prolonged his bewildered vigil, he chanced to notice someone familiar. Though, while he watched, he realized it had nothing to do with chance. Captain Alexei was out there, winding through the chaotic crowd... on his way -- clearly – for Horus' car...

Soon enough, he ducked into the shadows, looking back to assure himself of anonymity. Seeing that everyone was thoroughly engaged with their own business, he climbed up and over the front railing of the car, and rapped on the door...

The door with the fine monograms...

Horus Templar – Public Defender

* * *

Horus studied the police captain from the moment Deborah let him through the door. He was pale, hunched, and haunted… 'flighty,' as it were. It took Horus only a split second to be sure Alexei wasn't in the same funk as the rest of St. Argonsburg. No, he had some problem over and above that…

"Thank you kindly, Ms. Boulevard," Alexei nodded to Deborah after hurriedly removing his police bobby, as if suddenly realizing how the door had come open some moments ago.

"You're welcome," she replied gently, clearly picking up on his subdued manner.

Alexei turned and gave Art a nod. "Mr. Mallard. Hello."

Art folded his arms. "Backatya, Sirens."

Horus was rather appalled. "Now, don't be rude, Art. It's not the Captain's fault you couldn't get your nails done today."

"Your nails done?" Alexei asked.

"That's right," Art answered huffily.

Alexei blinked. "But… isn't that very girly?"

Now, Art had had it. He pointed what truly was a conspicuously overgrown claw right in the Captain's face. "Listen, buster… they don't call it a ***man***icure for nothing!"

"Never mind him, Alexei," Horus excused his big investigative friend. "Can I help you?"

Alexei nodded, thankful to have his attention drawn back to where he'd intended it. "Yes, thank you, Mr. Templar. That is… I hope you can. I'm in a spot of trouble, you see… the dynamics of which are proving, well… rather difficult to postulate."

"It seems to be the day for it," Horus joshed. He sat himself behind his desk and gestured for Alexei to take the seat opposite.

Alexei sat uncomfortably. "Well, I'm afraid I do get ahead of myself, Mr. Templar, Sir. There's actually official department business to discuss first. But then, that business and my business are all quite jumbled up together. So, well, perhaps I should just start from the beginning…"

"Please do," Horus invited him.

Alexei tried shaking some sense into himself. "Right, yes. You see, this morning, we apprehended a fleeing suspect. Which, I suppose, would be fine enough... except for one thing. The suspect turned out to be an Inquisitor."

Horus didn't react outwardly, except to freeze. "An Inquisitor. Well, now I've heard everything."

Alexei shook his head. "But I haven't told you the half of it yet, Sir."

Horus slid back in his chair, pensively joining his fingers. "What's the charge?"

"Only the latest. We picked him up on one very serious charge of illegal use of money."

Money, Horus privately reeled. The absolutely, positively, *most* unlikely crime for an Inquisitor. "And... your personal involvement?"

Alexei hesitated. "It seems... in the process of apprehending the Inquisitor... I shot him."

Horus let a long, exasperated sigh escape as he rubbed the flanks of his nose just beneath his eyes. "This is all rather a lot to take in."

"Oh, I sympathize, Mr. Templar, believe me." He shot a distant look out the window. "The big city life continues to baffle me at times. To be quite honest, Sir, it's putting a strain on my relationships. Whenever I write back home to Podunkville, I despair to juggle so many lies of omission. They would think me quite warped, if I told them about dueling Mantids, shooting Inquisitors, or consorting with Public Defenders... I hope you'll take no offense, Sir."

"I understand," Horus assured him. "But perhaps we'd better dispense with personalities for the moment. You have an Inquisitor in custody. Am I to represent him?"

Alexei nodded. "Yes, that is the official department business I spoke of."

Horus leaned in. "I suppose that begs another question. Am I legally permitted to *accept* a job, under present circumstances?"

Alexei nodded even more emphatically. "Oh yes, I'm almost certain, Sir. After all, it's not as if we intend to *pay* you." He blanched again. "That is, not before it becomes legal again."

"Fair enough. But you also mentioned business of your own. What of that?"

Alexei's features were once again contorted with fear. "Well... I was hoping you might be able to represent me, too. I can't begin to imagine the trouble I might be in, Mr. Templar. To harm an Inquisitor... what more offensive thing could a man do?"

Horus grinned, though he felt pity. "Much as I'd jump at the prospect of managing three clients at once, I'm afraid I can't help you, Alexei. For an attorney to represent both shooter and shootee would be one of those classic breaches of conflict of interest."

Alexei's dread sunk into a kind of dejected surrender. "Oh."

"...But don't fret. If things happened quite as you say, I'm certain the Inquisition won't begrudge you. They are eminently concerned with the proper carriage of duty. You did yours. You may be sure they'll respect that."

The captain perked back up. "Oh, thank you, Mr. Templar. Thank you very much." He sighed, wiping his face with a handkerchief. "I haven't breathed easy once since the incident. Not before now."

Horus stood from his desk. "Don't concern yourself about it any further. From what you've told me, it's my actual client who should be worried. For him to pay with cash would necessarily dictate he'd been in *possession* of cash to begin with... and for an Inquisitor, there's no greater trespass. It sounds like I'll have my work cut out for me."

"Are we going to meet this Inquisitor now?" Deborah asked.

"Yes," Horus replied, snatching up his briefcase, exchanging filled-out forms for blank sheets. "Do you mind going ahead and signaling a cabby?"

"Actually, yes," she answered.

Horus sighed, catching up with himself. "Right. I guess we'll just walk..."

Chapter 4

In the brief time it took for Horus to check in at the SAPD, he managed to lull himself into a false sense of normalcy. He exchanged customary greetings with Muriel, the receptionist, while busy policemen bustled in and out of the lobby, stirring the resident smell of stale doughnuts and strong coffee. By the time they finished filling out a guest pass for Art (who had insisted on coming, though he kept his reasons to himself), the oddities of the day were apparently left to the outside world. But just as Horus and company were all about to proceed to the detention area, Muriel stopped him...

"Oh, I nearly forgot," she said, reaching under her desk and producing an armful of big, blunt sticks wrapped in cloth on one end. "You'll need these in there."

Horus examined her proffered sticks questioningly. "Torches?"

"Oh yeah," she nodded. "See, it just so happens that we're nearly out of lamp oil right now, so we have to conserve it until we can buy more. There isn't any light in the holding cell area at all. That is, except what you bring with you." She held out the torches insistently.

Horus took one rather hesitantly, feeling like the subject of a prank. Deborah was quick to pluck the next one, even thanking the receptionist. But Art hung back...

"No thanks," he said. "I don't fancy wandering around in the dark with all the homicidal maniacs. Too spooky."

Deborah gave him a huffy look. "You're going to back out? Just like that? After all the trouble you went through filling out that guest pass?" Playful sarcasm tugged at her jowls.

"Come on, Art," Horus went along. "What's a little darkness? It's not like they went ahead and opened all the cells, too." In a moment of doubt, he turned to Muriel. "Did you?"

"No, that would be silly," she explained.

With a firm answer, Horus and Deborah eyed Art expectantly. At length, he groaned his assent...

"Fine. I'll come too. But know this: The moment anything creepy happens, I'm giving you both the ol' twenty-three skidoo."

"Fair enough." Horus beseeched the receptionist one last time, indicating his unlit torch. "Can you spare a match?"

* * *

In Art's defense, it *was* rather spooky in the detention area. Holding needlessly dim and flickering torches out against a total darkness filled with cages might have honestly been less unnerving if they were exploring some ancient dungeon, long bereft of living occupants. Instead, many of the cells they passed had *people* in them... sitting up, alert... perhaps looking even more shell-shocked than Horus began to feel, at the sight of them...

"First my nails, now this," Art bemoaned. "A guy can only take so much."

"I might feel a bit better, myself," Deborah said, looking up at Horus, "if I thought we had any idea where we were going."

Horus chuckled nervously. "I suppose I carelessly assumed there would be an officer on duty down here who could direct us to the proper cell. But so far, ours appear to be the only torch lights."

"I think we've been had," Art ventured, making a conspicuous sniffing sound. "If there was a lizard down here, I should have got a whiff of him by now."

"It's a big jail, Art. Don't make this into some kind of conspiracy." Horus did his level best not to further entertain his *own* conspiracy theories...

"Maybe we'd fare better if we split up," Deborah suggested.

"Yes, that seems the natural thing to do," Horus agreed.

"That's not even funny," Art protested.

Even as they considered the plan, they came to a fork in the path. "It's no joke," Horus said. "We need to find this Inquisitor. Anyway, it seems we've hit a crossroads. How about you and Deborah go this way, and I'll go that?"

Before Art could form another objection, Deborah spoke. "Don't worry, Art... I'll protect you."

Art sighed. "This isn't what I had in mind when I fancied a stroll in the dark with a beautiful gal. But oh well... no one lives forever."

At his prompt, Art and Deborah joined arms, starting down the wing of cells leading to the right. Horus found himself absently watching them go, before he finally turned his own way...

The slow steps of his small shoes echoed into the blackness ahead of him. He was obliged to wave his torch over every cell as he passed it, carefully scanning each one, only to confirm it was empty. After the first dozen cells proved to be quite vacant, he nearly turned back. But some sense or instinct urged him on… assured him that *something* was waiting for him, at the end of the path…

Finally, without so much as a thought, he stopped. He'd stepped over some invisible threshold – triggered a mutual awareness. He heard a latch… a swinging creek… and then a slam…

For a lengthy interval afterward, he heard nothing more… least of all the sound of his own breathing. Then, a voice prevailed in the dark…

"Well hello, Councilor. Fancy us meeting again so soon… over another injured client of yours, no less. Do you see how misfortune surrounds you? I wonder how long before it reaches in and lays hold of you, yourself."

Horus suppressed his reflexive start well enough. But as recognition dawned on him, he had a harder time suppressing his displeasure at this unwanted rendezvous…

"Hello, Doctor," he called back, sounding passably congenial. "I might've expected to run into you here. This does seem to be my year for exotic and badly-wounded clients."

The phantasmal voice took form before Horus as the vague outline of a Heron stalked into the torchlight. "The injury was not so grievous, I fear," Dr. Nokkaeru sighed. "And as for the 'exotic' nature of your client, you are bound to be disappointed. I certainly was."

"What do you mean?" he asked as she came to a stop. Even seeing her clearly now before him did not assuage his unease. The fire burned fiendishly in the goggles of her mask…

"You are expecting an *Avarican*, are you not?"

He nodded. "That's the customary persuasion of an Inquisitor." His ears twitched as he was confronted with the implication. "Do you mean to say this one is something else?"

"That *is* what I mean," she answered, assuming a blank stare into nowhere. "When I heard that a wounded Inquisitor had been taken, I dropped everything and rushed over. Rare indeed have been my opportunities to ply my instruments on Avarican physiology. They are maddeningly robust creatures, and equally stubborn to accept any kind of medical aid. To operate on one is a coveted benchmark for any Plague Doctor. So, you can imagine my displeasure, when I arrived at the cell… only to learn the patient was merely a Human."

Horus blinked. "A *Human*? That *is* unexpected. Granted, it's not unheard of. Not entirely… but…" He cut himself off as another layer of the mystery dawned on him. "But they told me he had *cash*… a *treasure*, so to speak.

What would possess a *Human* Inquisitor to hoard a treasure? There's no biology to stake that foible on..."

"If you are looking for a meaningful assessment of his psychological defects, you will have to consult a different doctor," she answered dismissively. "I will say this much in favor of his personality, however... his ascetic guilt complex has produced in him quite the glutton for punishment. When I had prepared to operate, he insisted that I remove the bullet without benefit of anesthesia. I was only too happy to oblige."

No doubt, Horus thought, straining to maintain a neutral expression. But after a moment's consideration, he was diverted by yet another puzzle. "You've already completed your work, then?"

"Yes. I sewed the final stitch not two minutes prior to your arrival."

Horus eyed her dubiously. "You'll have to excuse my curiosity, but these aren't exactly ideal surgical conditions." He indicated the torch in his hand. "There's no light at all in here but what I brought myself. Did your own torch burn down?"

"I had no torch," she intoned. "You recall, I was most displeased to learn my patient was of commonplace stock. I have always maintained that Humans are such simple creatures, I could operate on one with my eyes closed. Having been led here in the dark, it occurred to me this was an expedient opportunity to finally back up my boast. In so doing, I at least emerge from this misadventure feeling not entirely cheated."

"I'm so glad for you," Horus replied, unsure whether he even sounded sincere anymore, and not much caring. "But what of your patient? Is he fit for me to speak with him now, or do you suggest I come back later?"

"He is conscious and alert," she assured him. "As I said, there was no anesthetic."

"I understand. But do you think he will *feel* up to talking, after such an ordeal?"

"Oh yes. No doubt, to discuss heavy legal matters after traumatic surgery will come as a great strain. But that is his mode right now, and his wish... inasmuch as I may presume to peddle in psychology. He feels he has erred mortally, and suffering is his only salve. I would say the sooner you go and pester him, the better."

"Very well," Horus said, already feeling a bit conflicted about how to represent such a client's best interests. "In that case, I bid you good day, Doctor."

She began to walk by him. "Good day to you as well, Councilor. Enjoy such times while you may." Her voice echoed back to him as she regressed beyond the reach of the torchlight. "But remember: Your clock is ticking."

* * *

After a moment spent shaking out the chill of another meeting with Doctor Nokkaeru – apparently, his self-appointed harbinger of grim fate – Horus pressed on to the end of the hall. As he advanced, he heard a new sound, like scratching. When he reached the final cell – torch extended – he found what he was looking for: a cloaked figure, stooped over and scrubbing the ground. Horus had a time trying to figure out why. Finally, he realized the man must've been trying to clean away some of his own blood – without even the luxury of seeing where on the ground he might have bled. If Nokkaeru's brief account hadn't been enough, Horus was now quite convinced that he was dealing with damaged goods. The Inquisitor didn't even seem to take any notice of the light... much less Horus himself as he stood there holding it. When it became obvious he wouldn't be otherwise acknowledged, he cleared his throat...

"Hello there," Horus said, defaulting to perhaps the most superb of all icebreakers. "I take it you're the Inquisitor."

There was no immediate answer, beside a break in the scrubbing. "I used to be," the man finally stated. Horus grimaced at the sound of his voice. It was a young voice, he could tell... certainly much too young to be so empty. But even as Horus pondered that one brief utterance – and how to answer it – the man continued. "May I ask... who you are?"

"My name is Horus Templar – I've been appointed as your attorney." He knelt to be on the level with his client – still hunched down, but no longer scrubbing. "What is your name, Son?"

"My name is Rythigaar." The simple answer seemed to pain him. Horus, however, didn't take it for granted. He hoped he would not soon forget what an impossible battle it could be, just to get a client's name...

"Nice to meet you, Rythigaar," Horus replied, trying to seem upbeat, for what it might help. "I suspect today hasn't been the easiest day for you... for many reasons. To suddenly run afoul of the law – when you've spent your life mostly operating above and outside of it – must be disorienting. I admit to feeling a bit overwhelmed by the dynamics of your dilemma myself. But in any case, we should start with the facts. Can you tell me what happened this morning?"

Rythigaar nodded, then shifted to sit upright. "You would already know about... about the *treasure*, I assume. That's the essential beginning of this whole calamity. About eight days ago, we were called on to put down a marauding Avarican rogue. I was part of the detail assigned to locate the hoard, like usual." He huffed. "They'd always considered me 'safe'... a handy scout for searching out the gold that might have proved too much of a snare for the others." His head hung low as he shook it. "There was little else they could ever depend on me for. Next to my brothers and sisters, I was always so tiny... frail... *weak*. In a fight with a rogue, I would've been nothing more than a convenient snack. Even peoples' furniture proved too much... I broke my arm once just trying to smash a small end-table. Yes, apart from... well, a bit of light delivery duty... I was really only good for one thing. One impossibly simple thing. And even there, I failed." Here he paused a long time, collecting himself. "You must think me mad, to be what I am... a *Human*... and take a treasure hoard."

Horus suppressed a laugh. He had to admit the whole thing was a bit canted. Avarica – the dragon-folk – were naturally drawn to treasure, as part of their esoteric life cycle. An Avarican with a treasure was a fundamentally different being altogether from one without. For as long as some portion of their treasure – however small – remained unclaimed by any other creature, the Avarican in question would essentially be immune to death. Even if their body was slain – or completely destroyed – they would only, *inevitably* regenerate at the site of their treasure. Not only that... they would come back even larger and stronger than before. That was the nature of their existence, as the Creators had fashioned it... back in the folds of time, when they were still trying to get a good handle on what they wanted *life* to mean, and be like. Humans, on the other hand, didn't arrive until much later... and while money was valuable and appealing to them, it wasn't strictly a part of their makeup. They were designed to live out a brief cycle and die, without known exception...

Inquisitors – traditionally Avarican – were another layer of the tale altogether. Remembering the covetous atrocities of their ancestors, the Inquisition began as a reformation of their species, each member eschewing all treasure with deep, religious fervor. That sort of resolution should have come much easier for a *Human* Inquisitor...

"I grant that the oddity of it didn't escape me," Horus said.

Rythigaar remained deeply thoughtful. "I don't know if the madness of a trespasser can be put to words. Perhaps it's best not to even try. The reasons would change nothing, regardless. The irrevocable fact is: That last raid... when no one was looking... I stashed a chest. From that dreadful... *loathsome* pile of blood-money, I had the audacity... the *hubris*... the unspeakable wickedness to take something for myself."

Rythigaar didn't volunteer anything more after that. That they had started out attempting to visit the events of earlier that day seemed to escape him. Horus sympathized. The man's pain was deep – affecting – so that Horus had a hard time remembering the relevant substance of the conversation himself...

At length, he gently nudged things forward. "I take it your, shall we say, *indiscretion*, didn't go undiscovered."

Rythigaar shook his head. "No. Last night, somewhere in the fourth watch, I was found out. And I fled. I fled like the weave of Time itself could come undone if I only ran fast enough. And for a while, I was just deluded enough to feel like I might actually be escaping something. It wasn't until I reached the docks that the futility of it hit me... in rather a dramatic way." He threw up his hands. "I couldn't rationalize that clerk, refusing to sell me a ticket on a ship. I started out simply writing a check, just like any Inquisitor would do. But he kept turning down the payment incoherently. I despaired. I dared to try the cash. He still refused. I offered double... *triple* the fare. He *still* refused. I turned the entire chest over on his desk. But he only called for the police." Here he paused again. "The rest you either know already, or can guess easily enough. But still, I'm left wondering: What reason did he have, to deny me that ticket?"

Horus began to explain with some private amusement. "It seems, in your flight, you missed a rather important development. The Czarina outlawed the economy this morning."

There was another silence. "Really?" Rythigaar finally asked, no doubt at a loss.

"Incredibly, yes."

The former Inquisitor puzzled over this. "That does begin to explain my incarceration. But what a coincidence. No! No... to call it a coincidence would be a conceit. It was surely a *reckoning*... deserved, ordained, and carried out."

Horus winced. "Forgive me: I understand the burden of your guilt must be very great... but... do you really believe that events on a national level were orchestrated merely to hold you accountable for your wrongdoing?"

"Not *merely*," Rythigaar explained. "I don't presume to be the sole reason that your Czarina would mandate her... *unorthodox*... new law. That would be an even worse conceit. But I have no doubt there is intention behind my reckoning here. The Creators may have withdrawn, but Purpose remains. My flight ended as it ought. I will flee no more, whatever comes."

"Well, you *are* behind bars, but I respect the sentiment," Horus quipped.

For the first time, Rythigaar sustained a look directly at Horus, his mask inscrutable, but his posture attentive. "Tell me, Mr. Templar, must I accept legal counsel? I mean no offense; I just fail to see what I have to gain from representation. I am guilty of the charges against me. Can I not simply accept my punishment?"

Horus shrugged. "I'm afraid I don't even know what punishment you're liable for yet. I haven't had a chance to study the new law exhaustively. In this country, though, you can generally expect execution. But I'm sorry to say you're stuck with me, regardless. No one in Jast-Madiir may represent themselves unless they have legal credentials. Even to plead guilty, you'll need me."

A stirring in the corridor behind him caught Horus' attention, and he turned around when he'd finished speaking. He quickly recognized Deborah and Art... who had evidently rounded up another familiar personality...

"Don't jump... it's just us," Art called. "We didn't find your Inquisitor... but we did find somebody of note."

"So I see," Horus said, nodding to the newcomer. "Hello, Hamilton."

"Horus," District Attorney Hamilton Blackforest nodded back. "I don't mean to interrupt; you'll have to stop by my office after you've finished with your client here." His tone was rather subsumed.

"I certainly will," Horus agreed. "I was hoping you or someone from your office could enlighten me on a few things."

Blackforest rubbed the back of his neck uncomfortably. "I'll certainly do my best. But as I say, I'd rather not eavesdrop. You know where to find me when you're done."

"Sooner than you think," Horus replied, even as Blackforest turned to go. "I've nearly finished here."

At that, Deborah got huffy. "Well, thanks for waiting up, Boss. Don't forget I'm *supposed* to eavesdrop on you. If word of this gets out, I'll be bumped down to second-greatest secretary in the world *like that*." She snapped for emphasis.

"Your secret's safe with me," Horus grinned. "I'll get you up to speed later." He turned back to Rythigaar. "There's just one other matter I'd like to touch on for the time being... a major complication. You're not just a fugitive, after all... you're a fugitive twice over. I can help you navigate your legal situation. But if the Inquisition comes to claim you, well... I'll frankly be out of my depth."

"That's quite alright, Mr. Templar," Rythigaar assured him. "I told you I am finished running, and I meant it truly. If the occasion were to arise, I'm certain I could face them again." He stood up in his cell, though it caused him conspicuous agony. "Getting them to face *me* will be a different matter altogether."

Chapter 5

After an unnecessarily moody dungeon crawl complete with manifold defeatist personalities, Horus appreciated the chance to retreat to the DA's lofty level of the department building, where a bright afternoon was pouring through plenteous nice windows. Work went on diligently here. With an eye for detail, however, Horus couldn't help noticing – and being deeply perplexed – by the way it appeared that all the secretaries were typing onto documents that were already completely filled out. When at last he asked about it, one of Blackforest's secretaries explained that, in order to conserve paper, they had all been instructed to type up their new documents on the blank lines of old, double-spaced ones. Upon learning this, Horus indulged his curiosity further, snatching a sheet from the desk... giving it a quick once-over... blinking while his eyes spun. He let Deborah have a look, but she only shrugged it off. "In a pinch, you can even triple-up," she claimed. Horus couldn't imagine what past moment of desperation might have ever forced Deborah into such a feat of line-spacing conservancy, but he didn't ask.

It wasn't long before Horus also noticed that Art – while physically present – had his mind elsewhere. But catching his gaze, which was fixed on a door across the office, there was really no mystery in it...

"Not thinking of calling on Blucille Cordon again, are you?" Horus ventured.

Art's eyes never left the door. "I just have to get through the five stages of rejection."

"Five stages of rejection?" Deborah asked – amused – perhaps never more so than when it came to Art's lovesick malaprops.

"Sure," Art insisted. "First, she turns you down because you're a stranger. Then it's because you're annoying. Then you're a bit of a creepo. After a while, it's just a matter of principle. But somewhere around the twelfth time you ask a dame out, they finally start to think it's sweet. The five stages of rejection."

Deborah put a hand on her hip. "Are you even going to pretend you didn't just make that up?"

"Nope," Art replied.

About this time, Blackforest came out of his office, looking rather impatient. "I couldn't help overhearing familiar voices in sidebar out here," he said, leaning on his own doorframe with folded arms, a bit of a wild look in his eye. "Can it wait? We really need to talk about this Inquisitor thing."

"We'll be right there," Horus answered. He turned to Art. "Are you going to sit-in, Art? Or do you need more time with the door?"

Art sighed. "It'll be there on the way out..."

* * *

The door to Blackforest's office practically slammed when Horus and company had seated themselves. Aggressive footfalls filled the sonic void that followed. Each step had a crispness to it... almost a clicking sound, as if Blackforest's razor claws had lanced right through the soles of his shoes. Horus waited for the DA to take his own seat behind his impressive desk, but the sharp profile of his nemesis blazed right past it, electing to pace the room, circling like a one-man wolfpack. Through it all, though, Horus sensed no aggression. Nothing more hazardous or foreboding than acute agitation...

They waited what seemed a long time for Blackforest to get things started. But every time he opened his jowls, nothing escaped his clenched fangs besides imperceptible grumbles. Horus saw he would have to take it upon himself to initiate the council... but even his wide arsenal of clever wisecracks failed him at need...

"Rough day?" he finally settled on.

Hamilton groaned, throwing a fist to his desk. "I don't even know how to begin to tell you... if that wasn't already clear. How could everything come unbolted so fast, anyway? Yesterday, things were fine. *Peachy*. And now look where we ended up. My office isn't just behind the eight-ball... it's hemmed in from every side. I'm *surrounded* by eight-balls!"

"I suppose you mean the new law," Horus surmised. He was met with a deadly sarcastic grin...

"How remarkably astute of you, Horus," Blackforest breathed. "It certainly isn't the least of my troubles. But suppose we discuss our common problem before we get into all that..." He finally helped himself to his own seat, resting his elbows in notches he'd taken out of the mahogany desk with his nails.

"The Inquisitor," Horus stated.

"The Inquisitor," Blackforest grumbled back. "The least likely culprit... the last one we'd want to bring in." He gave Horus another fiery look. "Do you know how many Inquisitors we've incarcerated over the course of my tenure here?"

"If I were to venture another exceptionally astute guess, I'd say zero."

Blackforest nodded. "Very good. Coincidentally, that's the exact sum of all the Inquisitors this department has held from the founding of St. Argonsburg to date. If it had been in my power, I would've sorely liked to keep it that way." He sighed, drawing back into his chair. "That's where you come in, Horus. We're depending on you to fix this for us." He suddenly waxed evasive. "*I'm* depending on you, if admitting it helps anything."

"Well, it seems I've become rather important of late," Horus couldn't help goading. "But what precisely are you depending on me to do?"

"To make sure this jurisdictional dispute goes the right way," he answered, eyeing a paper on the corner of his desk. "Ms. Boulevard, would you kindly examine that letter in front of you?" He pointed at it. "Just there."

She snatched it up, reading double-fast. When her darting eyes were quite low on the page, Horus inquired. "What is it?"

"Priority correspondence from the local Inquisition Outpost," she said. "A reply to a message from this office about the runaway Inquisitor." Concluding her read, she set the letter back down and gave him a quizzical look, her ears set back. "They claim all their people are accounted for."

"You begin to see what a fix I'm in now, Horus?" Blackforest asked. He shook his head. "Frankly, I can't even make sense of it. He claims he broke the very strictest rule of their Order. We offer to extradite him... but rather than bring him to account themselves, the Inquisition tries to make like nothing happened. Am I missing something? Is it... is it even possible the man is merely an imposter?"

"No," Horus resolved.

Blackforest searched him. "You're absolutely sure of that?"

He nodded. "If you talked to him yourself, you'd be sure of it, too."

"As a matter of fact," the DA admitted, "I haven't had the pleasure."

"You didn't take his deposition?"

"He wanted it in writing," Blackforest explained, his eyes straying to his desk again. "His own."

"Here it is," Deborah announced, taking another document off the desk and handing it to Horus. He took it and skimmed, flipping through numerous pages...

"Poetically, *achingly* sorrowful," he summarized aloud. "This alone should have convinced you he was a trespassing Inquisitor."

"But a written deposition like that could have been carefully prepared and memorized ahead of time," Blackforest cautioned him. "Still, with your assurance the penitence holds up conversationally, let's just say he *is* an Inquisitor. What then? How do you account for the official statement from his Outpost that they aren't missing any personnel?"

Horus grunted. "That *is* a puzzle. One that will require some investigation." He put the deposition down to look Blackforest in the eye. "In the meantime, I need to know what you plan to do with him."

Blackforest chuckled. "*Me*? Why nothing. Nothing at all. As much nothing as possible, in fact... except to ship him back to his Outpost, the moment you get things cleared."

"But the *law*," Horus reminded him. "He *did* break a state law... one I admit I'm not much acquainted with as yet. What is the penalty to be paid for that? Execution, I suppose..."

"That's just it, Horus!" Blackforest despaired, claws upturned. "That's the whole second layer of this thing! Never mind the department doesn't need the black mark of *convicting* an Inquisitor, on top of apprehending one. But that blasted '*law*' came down from the Czarina's office no better than half-drafted! Sure, the economy is banned. But you asked the operative question: *How is the law to be enforced*?!" He left off there, toothy jaw jarred open as he panted.

"...Well?" Horus asked finally, not much appreciating the suspense.

"It doesn't say!" Blackforest growled at him. "There's no provision... no language anywhere in the thing that prescribes a sentence for illegal use of money. We have no idea what to do with him!"

"Hm..." Horus contemplated. "You do seem to be in something of a bind, my friend. But I'm not entirely sure what you expect me to do about it. As Mr. Rythigaar's attorney, representing his best interests, the last thing I should do is pressure the Inquisitors to pursue charges against him, if they would otherwise prefer not to."

Blackforest shook his head. "I'm not asking you to do that. But for the sake of record – and my sanity – I hope you will at least seek out their side of things... and let me know what they have to say for themselves."

"That sounds fair, on the surface. But what assurances do I have that you won't use what I find to try and persuade the Inquisitors to handle this matter internally?"

"None whatever," Blackforest admitted.

Horus grinned. "Alright. Since you'll only find out regardless, I'll see what I can unearth and let you know." He stood to go. "But there's one other thing," he said, reaching back down to the desk and retrieving the deposition. "May I keep this?"

Blackforest nodded. "Anything you want, if you think it can help, Horus. I'll have that copied and sent to you straight away."

"I'd thank you to do that," Horus replied, handing the deposition back to the DA.

"Just see to it I have reason to thank *you*." Blackforest slumped, looking downright bleary. "And the sooner the better."

* * *

Horus left Blackforest's office feeling rather mentally drained himself, trying to make sense of all the topsy-turvy details, but coming up well short of a complete picture. Why *would* the Inquisition try to dodge accountability for one of their own – the very Order who made it their business to be accountable for practically everything? In particular, he remembered Rythigaar's own statement... the oblique one he'd made at their parting, where he actually asserted it would be a job getting the other Inquisitors to face him. What did he *really* mean by it? What did he know, that Horus couldn't so much as infer?

These questions so preoccupied him that he didn't notice Blucille's door was now open. Nor did it immediately register when, just as Art was passing by, she happened to come barreling through it...

"Whoa!" Art said, quite startled himself as the ADA nearly ran into him. She only noticed an obstacle at the last moment, reflexively flinging a stack of documents when she came to a screeching halt. Both of them temporarily disappeared into a rain of paper...

"Say, I hoped I'd run into you here, Blucille, but this is a bit on-the-nose," Art said, both of them now rifling on the ground to corral her scrambled paperwork.

"*Really*, Mr. Mallard," she huffed. It took her a while to formulate a more concrete objection. She started to crease some of her own documents as her paper-snatching became more aggressive. "Our meetings are becoming gratuitous. I've already told you I won't be going with you to the opera."

"I remember," Art replied. "But that's old business. How about not going to dinner with me instead?"

She groaned. "You do realize I'm extremely busy? I'm not just carrying these papers for my health." She hesitated, taking inventory. Then she held out a hand. "Give me those there."

Now Art hesitated, papers in each hand, and her not giving him any cue which ones she was talking about, her eyes customarily buried – veiled beneath her downturned hat.

"In your *left* hand," she finally indicated, just as he had nearly settled on the right...

"I suppose that means you won't be going to dinner, then," Art ventured as she took her papers from him.

"You're not *listening,*" she said through her teeth. "I'm not trying to say I *won't* go. I'm telling you I *can't* go. I'm working ten different lawsuits right now! There is absolutely no place in my schedule for anything frivolous."

At that moment, Blackforest came back out of his office. Blucille hurriedly stood as if called to attention, fortunate not to sprain an ankle on her platform heels...

"Mr. Blackforest," she acknowledged him, voice unsteady. She didn't exactly relish looking like a clutz in front of her boss...

"Blucille," he replied, seeming rather dumbfounded himself. He wasn't accustomed to his understudy having emotion... let alone appearing on the verge of a furious meltdown. "Those financial suits you've been working... the businesses with the missing funds..." he snapped while he tried to remember something, "what was there: something like a dozen of them?"

"Ten, Sir."

"Right," Blackforest nodded. "Anyway, they've all been suspended."

She blanched. "Suspended?"

"Yes, every one of them. Shelved until the Czarina reinstates the economy. The justice department doesn't see much use in pursuing account imbalances while there are no accounts."

Blucille hesitated. "I understand. But surely you don't expect me to..."

"...We need to comply with the *law*, Ms. Cordon," Blackforest interjected. "Inasmuch as we can feel-out how to do it, that is," his gravelly voice half-grumbled. "If the courts have seen fit to put a freeze on this, then I intend to demonstrate full cooperation."

"But..."

"...You still have plenty on your plate. Why not memorize the rest of those transcripts I had shipped over from Cape Deltrix?"

"I already did, Sir," she admitted uncomfortably.

Blackforest raised a brow. "Oh."

The whole office felt dense with silence for a moment afterward, as Cordon and Blackforest pondered their impasse...

"...In that case," Blackforest began at length, "just... try to look busy for the rest of the day." He studied her... arms around a disheveled mass of papers... face looking aghast. "Honestly, this may be the best thing for you, Blucille. You seem a bit high-strung. Maybe try to get in some R&R. You could use it." He turned back for his own office, muttering audibly: "*We could all use it*," just before his door slammed.

Art looked at Blucille. Hesitantly, she looked back... bracing for the inevitable question...

"So... does that mean dinner's on?"

She forced another breath past firmly interlaced jaws. "Well in light of being *ordered* to relax and enjoy myself, I suppose I have little choice."

Art smiled radiantly. "That a girl! You won't be sorry, Blucille... I'll show you a swell time! Swanky dining... dancing... followed by even more grub! It'll be a real night on the town!"

Blucille approached him, a congenial grin on her own face, belied by eyes filled with something like thinly veiled rage. "Sounds like a *bash*. But I wonder how you intend to achieve all this, in lieu of the economy." She snatched the other handful of paper away from him.

Art's gleeful expression curled down nervously. "Well... I've got a few ideas about that. Never mind the details for now; I want it to be a surprise. Can I pick you up here? Er, that is... can I *meet* you here?"

"Here's as good a place as any. What time?"

"Say, quarter of 20:00?"

Her eyes narrowed dubiously. "It'll be a miracle if I'm hungry that early." She shrugged. "But whatever."

"Music to my ears!" Art elated. "See you then!"

"Inevitably," she agreed, giving him one more look up and down. "But if it's not too much to ask... could you at least show up properly groomed?"

Art blanched, remembering his nails. "Right... sorry! I was going to get these things filed down today, really. But you know... the economy and all..."

"Of course," she said, beginning to back away. "Good day, Mr. Mallard."

In the process of a wave, Art backed over a secretary's desk, narrowly avoiding another big, oafish spill. Blucille held a neutral expression while she slowly turned away...

* * *

They were waiting in ambush for him in the shadows of the doorway.

"That was an awful long chat for a simple 'no'," Deborah said.

Art shook his head. "There wasn't any 'no' this time. She said *yes*!"

Deborah blinked. "*Really*? What on earth would make her say something like that?"

"Her boss," Art blurted before half-thinking about it. "Er, well, mostly it was my charm and dashing good looks. But being conveniently out of work and excuses also helped."

"Well, congratulations, Art..." Horus said, "...but don't let it go to your head. I'm going to need you at your best this afternoon. There's investigation to be had."

"Right," Art sighed, dutifully taking mental inventory. "You were telling me earlier that the State wanted you to take a look at about a dozen accounting cases...?"

Horus exchanged a look with Deborah. "...That's right. Blucille asked me to look into it... even to enlist your help, if necessary."

Art got a bit excited again. "You mean, she *mentioned* me?"

"Yes, but only under duress," Horus explained. "The thing is, Art..." he started in a suspiciously gentle way, "...the accounting job is looking to be nothing but a straightforward paper trail, at present. Books and bank statements. I'm confident Deborah and I can handle it. I have something else in mind for you..."

After a moment of thought, Art smiled mischievously, like he was being put on. "Oh, that's rich. You're about to tell me I'm being put on the Inquisitor job. You want me to go to their base and chat it up with the scary lizards. Right?"

Horus' expression didn't change. Art's began to droop...

"Now wait a minute. You're not seriously..."

"...I'm afraid so, Art. Like I say, your talents of observation will be wasted on the accounting job. But you were there for Blackforest's brief: The Inquisitors maintain they have no missing personnel. Something's amiss here: By default, there's some level of disinformation or coverup already at work. That's why I'd really feel better sending you."

Art stumbled over a whole minefield of objections, just trying to pick one to start with. "But Horus... you've already been to that place. You've already rubbed elbows with one of their bigwigs. You've got pull there. Shouldn't *you* be the one to go?"

Horus shook his head. "When they learn I sent you, that should be credit enough… if, indeed, Inquisitors pay any mind to such things."

"But why do you even *need* to go over the accounting right now? Blucille just got taken off those cases… they've been suspended while the economy's out…"

"All the more reason to pounce on it now," Horus argued. "I hate to misuse gifted time."

"What's the matter, Art?" Deborah goaded. "Still worried the Inquisition will find out about that nice new fishing boat of yours?"

"Among other things," Art nodded, before promptly returning his attention. "Horus, give it to me straight… do I *really* have to go? I don't think I'm a good fit for this assignment at all. I'll be a nervous wreck!"

Horus shrugged. "Well… at least that guarantees you'll be alert. I'm sorry Art, but this is the way the chips have fallen."

"Right," Art huffed. "Thanks for the customary sympathy… though I'd rather do without."

"I'll make it up to you somehow, if I can," Horus assured him.

"I'll hold you to that." Art had a thought, producing his hands for his own inspection. "In fact, there *is* something you might do for me…"

Chapter 6

"*Achk*! Careful, Horus! Nails have nerves in them, you know."

Horus grimaced, fumbling to capture Art's recoiling hand again. "Oh, I'm aware. In fact, I'm not entirely sure your nails are made of anything *but* nerves."

"Are you even buffing with the grain? It's important to buff *with* the grain, not against it."

Deciding that he couldn't stand to trifle with the pointer nail any longer, Horus moved on to the next finger, having not the slightest idea or care what 'the grain' was, much less which way it might be going. "You're such a trove of trade secrets," he grumbled, "I wonder why you don't file these things yourself."

"I only know what the pros tell me," Art explained. "I've never actually witnessed the process myself."

Horus could only roll his eyes, looking down at the reclined form of his big investigatory friend. It was not a discrete eye-roll. Nor did he have any reason to wonder why Art had never seen his nails done before. When the question had been put to Horus about being Art's manicurist for the day, he'd asked in return – with what he'd thought was obvious sarcasm – whether, as part of a broader salon experience, Art would also like some of those cucumber slices for his eyes...

"Boy, would I!" Art had answered. "Do you really think you could get some?"

Horus laughed... at first... until it began to slowly dawn on him that Art was stone serious. This began a brief and highly improbable scavenger hunt through the SAPD pantry. The closest Horus got was a summer squash. But rather than return empty handed, he decided to go with it. It had been his hope that, with a little sleight-of-hand, he could apply the squash slices without Art ever noticing the difference...

The other, more important tool to the project, Horus had experienced no trouble procuring. For by a strange and rather unaccountable coincidence, what the police department lacked in cucumbers, they more than made up for with a vast wealth of nail files...

So now, here they were – attorney and private eye – grooming and being groomed. It was perhaps an equally hazardous experience for both. Horus nearly cut himself on an overgrown claw just trying to get a better grip – one he hoped Art couldn't so easily muscle out of the next time he got spooked about his nerves... which only happened about every second brush of the file. Finally, he realized he needed something to divert Art's attention – perhaps just a spot of conversation. Yes, that seemed the professional thing to do...

"So, you seem pretty serious about Blucille. I hadn't supposed weeks ago that you would keep on after the first few rejections."

"Oh, come on now. I'm the kinda guy who goes steady... you know that. I don't ask a gal out once if I don't already have my mind made up that she's worth asking a dozen times or so." His hand flinched a little, but Horus didn't let it get away. Already, this was a sign of improvement. Maybe after a bit more chatting, he could try his luck with the side of the file that had the deeper grooves...

"You'll pardon me being very frank: I'm not entirely sure what you see in her, Art. She is brilliant and attractive, I grant. And I do suspect that, deep down, there are the seeds of a caring soul in her. But if she's very determined to keep them buried – as she certainly seems to be – then I don't know what you're going to be able to do about it. I'm not sure I've ever met anyone more emotionally closed-off in my life... more determined to avoid engaging in the moment. I suppose if you could get her to open up a bit, it would probably be the best thing for her. But it has all the earmarks of being quite the uphill battle. I just hope you aren't too smitten to see what you might be up against."

Art shrugged. "Maybe I like a challenge. Maybe that's part of what I find interesting about her." His voice got low and thoughtful. "Who knows? Maybe all it will take to bring her into the moment is to convince her someone wants her there. Maybe she just needs to see that someone's interested in finding out who she is."

Horus was rather taken aback. He'd considered Art a friend for some time, but in the moment, he had to admit that his knowledge of the man didn't venture far beyond the professional sphere. Apparently, under all that bulk, there was a tender heart. Perhaps almost as tender as the ends of his fingers...

"Well, I hope your instincts serve you well, Art. But do be careful. Someone who's buried their feelings as deeply as she has could just as easily be very indisposed to having them dug up." He arrived at a sensitive question. "You... you haven't checked into her background at all, have you? Her past?"

"Nah, nothing like that," Art replied. "Granted, that's what I do for a living... but this is personal. I don't wanna know anything she doesn't feel like telling me herself. Or, well... even *if* I wanna know, I at least have the discretion not to go snooping."

Horus was relieved by his friend's good judgment... even as he suddenly felt a pang of another anxiety...

"I'm glad to hear it. However, since you brought up *discretion*, maybe it would be best if we didn't further pursue these subjects in present company..."

The two of them were, in fact, still in the lobby of Civil Headquarters.

"There's no one here right now but Muriel," Art argued. "I'm sure she hasn't even been listening."

"Not a word," Muriel agreed.

"Very well," Horus went along. "Though I don't know what more there is to say. I think you have a fine hypothesis about Ms. Cordon... but beyond my hope, I can hardly speculate as to its accuracy."

Art lifted a squash with his free hand. "Listen to you, Horus. I'm down here trying to have a heart-to-heart, and you're carrying on like some kind of scientist." He huffed. "*Accuracy. Hypothesis*. Maybe Blucille's not the only one with emotional retention problems. I'm talking about *feelings*, Horus."

Being successfully on to the third fingernail, Horus invited him to continue. "Alright. If you have more on the subject, go ahead. What are you *feeling*?"

Art sighed, trying to put words to it all. "I dunno. Maybe I'm just lonely. Only it feels like something that goes beyond that. Like maybe there's *supposed* to be more to life. It seems like there must be. I can't think of any other reason to be unhappy. I mostly enjoy the work I do. I like poking my nose into people's business and figuring stuff out. I make a lot of dough at it, too... and I've become quite the hand at spending it. But it all just sort of leaves me flat these days. Not like Blucille. She makes me feel..." he began, really straining for just the right word. "She makes me feel..."

"...Inconsequential?" Horus blurted.

"Right!" Art agreed enthusiastically. "Like, almost non-existent! Just a petty nuisance, at the best of times."

Horus made a face. "And you... like that?"

"Sure do," Art said. "It's like I said earlier... I must dig a challenge. It's obvious I don't matter to her at all. But if I can change her mind about me... man, that would really be something."

It was about this time that Horus flipped the file over, moving on to the pinky...

"*Yow*!" Art said. "Careful of the little one!"

"This wouldn't be so painful if you'd just stop squirming," Horus chided him.

"I wouldn't squirm if it wasn't so painful," Art argued.

Horus belabored a great sigh. "Why me, Art? Don't you think Deborah could have handled this just as well?"

"Certainly no worse," Art quipped. "But come on, Horus. It's not like I could talk with her about lady stuff, like I can with you."

"You don't think so? She might just have some knowledge on the subject..."

"You know what I mean. She'd just give me a hard time like she always does."

"About like I've been doing."

Art snorted. "Yeah, yeah."

For a little while, neither of them said anything more. Much as Horus might have appreciated the silence, the need to distract Art from his overacting tactile senses remained paramount. But he'd only just begun to consider how to change the subject when Art surprised him...

"What about the two of you, Horus? You and Deborah, I mean?"

That gentle, unassuming question froze Horus like a blast of liquid nitrogen. And just as well, too... for if he had forced himself to move through its asking, he would have certainly slipped the file and chipped half the nail off. Always a man of composure, he didn't let himself be tripped up long. He *couldn't*... if he meant to maintain the façade of indifference he'd found so important to cultivate over the last few years, for whatever reason...

"What about us?" he asked gruffly, hoping to sound more unhappily engaged in the task at hand than the question itself. He was only glad Art couldn't see him sweat... though, of course, he couldn't sweat...

"I dunno. I always kinda thought the two of you would make a sweet pair... a really great team, ya know?"

Horus snickered, perhaps despite himself. "Well, we *are* a great team... even if I still lose my share of cases."

Art hesitated. "So, that's it, then? Purely professional? I know you don't need me to tell you what a special lady she is: smart, hard-working, world-renowned, cute as a button, a sarcastic streak only rivaled by your own... with a smile and a punch in the arm for any malaise. I've seen her coach you out of the dumps more than once. You mean to tell me you've never thought about asking her out?"

Unwittingly, and quite against his will, Horus had tumbled head-first into one of those impromptu crossroads in life, where the entire future of the cosmos seemed to hinge on how you chose your next words. Whether he had time for it or not, he lost himself, deep in the swirling vortex of calculation. What did he have to lose, admitting the truth here? Art was a friend... and apparently, a would-be confidant, who had just spent the last several minutes sharing his own personal baggage. And what would he really be confessing to? The question was so minor... so harmless: Had he ever – even *once* – given a passing thought to taking Deborah out on a simple date? Surely, it couldn't hurt to admit to *that* much...

"No," Horus said.

And thus, Horus had sealed his fate... or so it felt – a self-described man of truth, caught in a reflexive lie. He was left to ponder many things. What had really stopped him up? Did he have some irrational fear that the merest hint of his true feelings for Deborah would somehow detract from their dignity, or their sense of reality? Was he really so proud... or so insecure? Or, was it not so much his fear of the question itself, but of the questions that would inevitably follow? That once he cracked the door open, Art would inevitably draw out the *whole* truth? Perhaps he was just too comfortable in the status quo. To broach the subject of his secret love for her would inherently start him reexamining the resolution he'd made: to content himself in their working relationship. What needless drama might ensue if he were to suddenly upend that applecart?

Moreover, would Art Mallard – famed investigator – actually *believe* the answer he just gave him? That worry quickly won out over the others, while he waited intently for the next thing Art would say...

"Huh," Art replied. "Well, that's kind of a shame. I figured a guy like you would have her pegged for a dreamboat. But I guess I'm no matchmaker after all."

Horus concealed his relief as best he could. Art's powers of perception proved fallible after all... just when he most needed them to. Perhaps the *only* time he'd ever needed them to...

"Even so," Art started back up, shifting in his chair while Horus circled around to the other hand, "I wish you both the best in your search for a soulmate."

"You're the seeker, Art. I don't see myself on the hunt any time soon."

"Ya never know, Horus. Ya never know. Love is in the air. All ya gotta do is wake up and smell the roses. Or, in my case, the lavender pipe soap." Art audibly sniffed, offering a contented sigh. "I've still got a whiff of it in my nostrils." He sniffed a few more times... unsure. "That... and summer squash?"

Chapter 7

The pampering just couldn't last. Any amount of time would have been too soon, of course, considering Art's next order of business. Whereas he'd whiled one hand worth of grinding under Horus' clumsy file talking about mushy stuff, he'd made sure to spend the other hand trying to whine and weasel his way out of this assignment. No such luck...

Presently, he set one of those hands over the inner pocket of his trench coat, where there was a special little something he'd just plucked from along the highland path, as if to remind himself of the light at the other end of this proverbial tunnel. But even the bliss of his impending date with Blucille could only be dimly glimpsed through the ominous gloom of his march beyond the outer shambles of the city, where he was to present himself at the drawbridge of a dark, grim fortress full of Inquisitors. He could see the horrible place now. Shadows lengthened with his every step, while stark metallic spires mounted to the very heights of his field of vision. Night was closing in on him, right along with everything else.

Soon enough, he found himself crossing a wide bridge over a long fall into spikey nothingness. An acidic smell plucked his nostrils, so that the hairs within stood as rigid as the ones along the back of his neck. He plastered on a grin for the source of the odor: rows of heavily-armed Avarican guards advancing, expressionless masks trained on him, each concealing what must have been an equally expressionless face. It was ironic, then, that while their heavy feet stalked past him, Art felt distinctly that he could read what their empty looks had to say. They said, in frightful, hushing tones: *"We know, Mallard. We know about the fishing boat. And the rest of the loot, too..."*

Before he had quite reached the end of the bridge, towering doors were opened in front of him, revealing a lone Inquisitor in his path. Her spindly, piercing fingers turned up and open toward him...

"Artimus Mallard, I presume?" the Door Keeper called. Art froze. It was rather uncanny: her knowing his name, and all. Truth be told, standing at the threshold of such an imposing doorway, and hearing his name called by some monastic sentinel... it felt a bit like being welcomed at the gates of Heck...

"Greetings," she went on, having to accept his stunned silence as confirmation of his identity. "Your arrival is timely. Primary Administrator Hihvnor will be with us presently. The matter at hand is a sensitive one, to be sure. Nevertheless, the Administrator is pleased to offer your esteemed colleague Horus Templar what assistance he may. Or, failing assistance, to at least offer transparency."

"You..." Mallard faltered, "...you knew I was coming?"

"Yes," the Door Keeper answered. "Word of your calling has reached us via carrier pigeon, from the secretary Boulevard."

Art sighed his relief. An earthly explanation after all...

"That's a real load off my mind," he admitted, though he just as quickly fell back into a measure of apprehension. "You said I'd be meeting with a Primary Administrator?"

"That is also correct. The Administrator has been in past conference with Mr. Templar. Regrettably, he was unable to be of measurable assistance in the matter of the Mantid case. For this reason, Hihvnor wishes to personally represent our position in this present ordeal... as a very minor token of his goodwill."

Art nodded nervously. "Okeedoke."

Much to his surprise and dismay, the Door Keeper and himself had, by this time, already come hard and fast to the very end of anything they had to say to one another. He stood there, sniffing, shifting on his feet, manually smoothing down the back of his neck, and trying to divert his attention to anywhere but the Avarican woman in front of him, whose perfectly stationary and statuesque gaze back at him unnerved him to no end. Inquisitors had always given him the willies, and not just because they were the oldest and most eminently powerful organization in the entire world... an orgainization which, among other things, made it their business to search out and destroy anything and everything a person could own that was remotely fun. No, part of his discomfort was certainly owed to their mere projection of presence. The off-putting smell. The creepy duds. And – worst by far – that dratted *motionlessness*, for which this Door Keeper was a poster child. While he waited in agony for, of all things, a *Primary Administrator* to show up, he felt distinctly that she could stand there with her hands interlaced and watch him in silence for an hour, a whole day, or even a week, and not think twice about it... much less flinch.

Finally, he could stand it no more. Though there was nothing to talk about, he needed to get the conversation rolling again, or he'd bust. Still looking all around, there was really only one thing to observe. He would have to make do with it...

"Some place you got here," Art finally said. "Very pointy. Very, *very* big."

"Indeed," the Door Keeper replied. "Yet you must not be over-impressed by what you see on the surface. The heights these towers reach pale utterly next to the depths we delved, in constructing this fortress."

Art's ears set as he wrestled with such a revelation. "Holy smokes. So we're talking *big*-big."

"And yet not over-engineered," she cautioned him. "We deplore excess."

"So I've heard. But then, if you don't mind my asking... what would make you want to build... so much?"

"This site first served as a very peculiar prison in a former age," she explained. "Surely you will have heard of the Great Regression, Mr. Mallard?"

But of course, he'd heard of history's leading cataclysm. It wasn't a subject lightly broached, even thousands of years later. But in his present state of unrest, any conversation piece at all might have suited him better than none...

"Yup. It's supposed to have been a doozy of a time."

"That it was. Our Order was quite beset with troubles in those days. Among them, few were greater than the false teachings of the heretic Galahadron Mucolyptus. His poison words swayed many to his Dark crusade, including Huytut, Queen of the Wuu Gappews."

Art whistled. "A Meduseldan Queen? That's quite a prominent follower."

"And an immensely large one. But yes, more than prominent, she was critically unique. The Inquisition could not very well allow her to follow the mad Galahadron through his Gate, and in so doing cut off from our universe one of the Seven Meduseldan Dominions – a staple of creation since its very origin. But we had this prison... a secret project from a few centuries prior, which we had hoped to use to detain the dread Queen Aedeloma. It went on to become the detention center for Huytut, and all manner of Galahadron's converts... those we were able to lay hold of, at any rate. But of course, it is a matter of record that Opepci and he went on to stage a very great exodus through the Gate they built, despite our best efforts."

"Still, at least you nabbed the Queen. How did you ever manage that?" It was also a matter of record that people didn't generally tussle with a Meduseldan Queen, much less with any success. Throughout all of history, only one had ever been killed... and then, of course, only briefly...

"It was rather easily done," the Door Keeper claimed. "We simply informed her that Galahadron's Gate was at the very bottom of the large pit we dug here, then closed the fortress over her." She shrugged. "Wuu

Gappews have always been notoriously impressionable. Her collusion with Galahadron in the first place confirms as much."

"Right," Art asserted, not much understanding, but certainly inclined to seem agreeable with whatever the Inquisitor had to say. To hear her speak was oddly affecting... very much as if she had been present for it all... which, was even just possible...

"Many long years have come and gone since then, of course," she went on. "Huytut reached the end of her span, as did most of the inmates here. Idruilthoronta was yet young in those days, and only in recent centuries has this outpost seen extensive use again, conveniently nestled astride the political and economic heart of your modern Jast-Madiir. But a prison it was founded, and a prison it remains. And we are well served to keep it as a contingency, should the need ever arise to detain another Meduseldan Queen."

Art allowed himself a small chuckle. "Kind of ironic. When you get right down to it, Rythigaar fled from one prison straight into another."

The Door Keeper hesitated. "Hm... yes. But let us not speak so directly of your business. It is Hihvnor who has accepted that burden, and not I."

"Well, okay," Art shrugged. This was yet another ironic turn. He certainly never imagined that, in the course of conversation, he'd somehow make the *Door Keeper* feel uncomfortable...

Before he could hope to relish the shoe being put on the other foot, however, a distant commotion pricked his well-tuned ears. It was a sound of marching feet... many *big* feet, with horrible long knives for toes...

"Ah, he comes," the Door Keeper explained, moving off to one side of the great doorway. "Now, all shall be made clear."

Art gulped. This Hihvnor was evidently not the only one coming out to greet him. It sounded like a whole platoon...

Sure enough, they were on him within moments – rows of Inquisitors issuing from the main door, as well as unseen access points on both sides. Art was surrounded in no more time than it took to catch a pitiful 'yelp' in his throat. Even the guards which had earlier passed him on the drawbridge had apparently doubled-back, cutting off his only escape. An owner of a strictly recreational watercraft – and so many really nice fancy things – Art's paranoia revived with a vengeance...

"Well hello, Mr. Mallard," another Inquisitor called, stepping out into the waning daylight. "I am Primary Administrator Hihvnor. I trust you were told that I should be your contact." He looked over his assembly of shock troops.

"But efficiency is a demanding taskmaster, and we find ourselves beset now with multiple errands, don't we, men?" They nodded. Hihvnor trained his look back on Art. "You will of course understand if our business takes us down to the *docks*? It is my hope that you will accompany us there, so that we may kill two birds with one stone, so to speak."

Art stood dumbstruck. This was it. They really *did* know. Somehow, they *really did know* about his fishing boat! And now, they'd come in force, dropping their ominous hints. They were about to have him lead them out to where it was tied up... then make him watch helplessly while they smashed it to splinters...

"The docks?" Art repeated timidly. "Well... I don't... I don't know if..." Finally, he forced himself to rally and ask a coherent question. "That is, what business do we have by the docks? It couldn't... perchance... be the business of breaking stuff?"

"Oh, yes... that it most certainly is," Hihvnor answered, coming right up and setting a big claw on Art's shoulder... sounding almost as if he were holding back a snicker. "But come now, Mr. Mallard. If your concern is for your fishing boat, then it is unfounded. We have not the time to trouble about it today."

This news came as no small relief. "*Really*? Gee, that's swell! I mean, you sure had me going there for..." His eyes bugged. "Wait... so you *do* know about the boat?!"

Hihvnor laughed a great, hearty, full-bodied laugh just over Art's face, nearly singeing his whiskers. "Mr. Templar's secretary has proven aright!" he announced. "Her message claimed we would get quite the rise out of you, if we were to make mention of a fishing boat!"

That Deborah, Art thought. He didn't mind so much that she was always giving him a hard time, but now she'd gone and taken it a bit too far. He'd have to get her back some time...

"...Oh, but then..." Hihvnor began again, as his mirth declined, "...if there truly *is* such a boat, you must know that we *will* find it, and destroy it... the next time your name comes up for purging."

Art snickered nervously. "Duly noted." He was really, *really* going to have to get her back...

"But come, I say," Hihvnor repeated, starting himself and his troops on the march. "Our errands beckon us onward. You and I shall have words on the way..."

* * *

"First thing we need to get straight, Mr. Hihvnor," Art said, feeling more confident behind the veil of his ubiquitous notepad as he and the Inquisitors descended on an unsuspecting coast. "You know well enough, I think, that the police have a man named Rythigaar penned up Downtown... a man that, by all appearances, is an Inquisitor. But the DA says your people told him they weren't missing anyone. Now, I don't mean to call you out, exactly... but well, last I checked, yours was the only base in town. Not only that: Your Door Keeper clammed right up the moment I mentioned our guy by name. This whole thing smells of some kind of cover-up. So what am I missing? How do I reconcile your statement to the DA with the facts of the case?"

Hihvnor sighed. "What a grim misfortune this is. I am only glad that you've come to hold us accountable for our deception. But you should know it was not our intention to deny the facts... only to deny the man himself. We are *not* missing one of our own... because, tragically... the man Rythigaar is no longer one of us."

"Because he took a treasure, you mean?"

"Yes."

"And that's your biggest no-no?"

"Far and away, it is."

"Despite the fact that treasure-hunting is bred into you guys... Avarica, that is. The Creators designed your race to stash gold away, become death-proof and grow into big scary dragons. But for some odd reason, you Inquisitors swear all that materialism off, even though you revere the Creators more than anyone. I never quite got that."

"Sometimes, I feel that is just as well," Hihvnor said. "The great onus of the Inquisition cannot be wholly in vain if those outside of it, such as yourself, may live in blissful ignorance of the perilous nuance between right and wrong. Yes, we were designed by the Creators to covet wealth. But where did the indulgence of that imperative lead? It led to an epoch of strife... it led to Onyxadon... to the Pirate Lords... to a thousand other dragons that once scourged the earth, whose names we have had the good fortune to forget. Worst of all, it was surely our greed which inspired the Creators themselves to depart, and to start their work anew, as far away from the memory of us as they might. So you see, we have much cause to reject our nature. It is hardly less than the root cause of all suffering."

"Fair enough," Art replied, finding his brain taxed by such a barrage of ontology. Being an investigator had, in his experience, tended more towards looking for shoeprints under magnifying glasses than trying to wrap one's mind around the vast, intangible truths of existence. "But Rythigaar... he doesn't precisely share that nature. He's just a Human. I mean, it's not like he could go on to become the next Onyxadon. Frankly, I can't even imagine what the little guy was thinking when he took that loot..."

"Nor can I... though it is not a matter I dare meditate on. But I will say this: Humans are a curious bunch. They learn so fast... as of course, they must. But they are excitable and impulsive creatures. I fear they never live long enough to overcome the follies of youth. I will admit, I regret that his sin cannot be acknowledged for its peculiarities... and so met with peculiar amnesty. But it cannot matter *what* he is. What is wrong for one Inquisitor must be equally wrong for all. I am in no place to make exception."

"I guess that explains your claim," Art said, scribbling down notes. "But it doesn't explain why you won't let the police extradite him back to you. He broke *your* rule. Why not deal with him yourself? The door lady said your base was a prison. So why keep him in the city jail?"

Hihvnor did not answer straight away, striding in thoughtful silence. "Your questions become progressively more difficult, Mr. Mallard. We have never *held* a trespasser. Nor have we... *dealt with* one."

Art grimaced. "You're kidding. Never?" Hihvnor had been honest to this point, and Art firmly believed he *remained* honest, even now. But the claim was incredible. "But surely Rythigaar isn't the first one to *ever* break your rule?"

"No," Hihvnor admitted. "There have certainly been many others. And yet, the story has always been the same. Each and every trespasser – from first until last – has fled away from us, in their shame and disgrace. They *flew*, just as fast as they could bear themselves away." Hihvnor turned his mask up to regard Mallard. "Rythigaar is merely the first to be *caught* in the act of fleeing."

"All the rest managed to get away?" Art asked, still incredulous.

"Yes, but that was no feat. We did not hinder them. We only turned away."

At last, things began to look clearer to Art. He was reminded at once of what he'd heard Rythigaar say, just as Horus and he were concluding their conversation: about how difficult it would be to get the other Inquisitors to face him...

"I see," Art replied. "You give 'em the silent treatment. But even there, I'm surprised. You guys put down other dragons just for having a treasure." He grew uneasy, trying to find a delicate way to arrive at his next question. "So, I guess I can't help wondering... if you've got one right in front of you... why you don't... you know... kinda nip it in the bud, so to speak?"

"You base that inquiry on a false assumption, Mr. Mallard. We don't actually 'put down' dragons for having a treasure. They are quite few in number, especially in this part of the world, but there are actually Avarica still living outside of the Inquisition, who are neither hunted nor hindered from participating in a commercial existence."

"Okay..." Art sighed, about ready to toss his notepad in the gutter, "...you lost me again."

"It is as you said before... to *have* a treasure is a part of our nature, as the Creators fashioned it. It is by far the most subjective area of the Inquisition's policy, but in some way, we feel obliged to remember that truth of our existence, and to make some allowance for it. Again, I say: We do not kill dragons for merely possessing a treasure. It is only once the *treasure* has possessed the *dragon* that we step in. When they can no longer conduct themselves personably – when the desire for spoils leads them to violence – only then do we react violently." Hihvnor put up his hands defensively. "It is not a perfect system, we understand. Certainly, we fall short of preventing mayhem by waiting for the dragon to make the first move. But we know no better way. For the young Avarican to truly choose the way of reformation, the other way must also abide. It must continue to play out tragically, as it invariably does, and so be seen for what it is."

"All this Inquisitor stuff is tricky," Art confessed. "For as much as I think I follow, every answer leads to another question."

"You may certainly go on asking," Hihvnor assured him. "I don't wish for you to return to Horus Templar feeling I have withheld any information from you. Especially since information is the very best I have to offer."

Privately, Art began to grow somewhat weary of all the insistence that the Inquisition – again, *the most powerful* organization in the world – could do no more here than dole out information. But before he could try to call Hihvnor out on it, a scout or other functionary from the squad of Inquisitors came up to her boss...

"Ah, hello, Giriyeedra," Hihvnor greeted her. "What news from the shipwrights?"

"They have received your instruction and are in process of compliance, Administrator," she answered with a nod. "Evacuation of the yards is under way, even now."

"Very good," Hihvnor replied, a sort of joyful exuberance returning to him with the apparently good news... whatever it actually meant. "And, the *Temperance*?"

"It is arrived, and within striking distance. The captain awaits your signal."

"Very good indeed. Return to the shipyards with all haste. We will be on your heels."

"Yes, Administrator." She turned and ran away.

Art flipped his notepad shut. "I guess pragmatism dictates my next question: What are we actually out here to do?"

"Ah yes," Hihvnor laughed, "I suppose I failed to mention the nature of this outing. We've come to perform our customary purging of excess... albeit on a grander scale than usual. Did you know, Mr. Mallard, that your Czarina has been constructing a new flotilla of not less than seven ivory warships?"

Art blanched. He certainly *didn't* know. "*Ivory* warships? You mean...?"

"...Yes, you do not misunderstand me: They are in fact made of pure ivory."

"The whole ship? Or, well, *ships*? All of them?!"

"All but the sails, the cannons, and some of the furnishings, according to the blueprints," Hihvnor answered.

"*Hot dog,*" Art let slip. "That must've cost a pretty penny."

"*Seven* pretty pennies, to be exact," Hihvnor corrected. "Which comes out to around six too many. The Czarina can be grudged a single ship of such make, if that is how she elects to allocate her military budget. But we must certainly destroy the rest."

Art continued to reel. "You're going to sink a bunch of the Czarina's ships? Tonight? When she's already hopping mad about the whole trade war thing going against her?"

"We are seizing the opportunity afforded by the suspended economy, yes. Since the shipwrights cannot be paid to continue their construction anyway, it seems the ideal time to undo their efforts so far."

"Still sounds like a raw deal to me," Art argued. "It's still illegal *not* to work, you know. But they'll be out of the job..."

"Not if we also destroy the berths," Hihvnor countered. "That will leave them with something they may rebuild."

"Ah, good thinking," Art assented.

"We try to be thorough. But now we must hop to it, Mr. Mallard," he said, progressing to a jog. "Let's get there and see if any help will be needed in the evacuation..."

* * *

Truth be told, Art fell a few steps behind in the impromptu marathon to the coast. He had a good physique for a pool-house brawl, but was wasted on cross-country. By the time he reached the royal naval yards, there were already huge lines of Humans standing on the boardwalk, looking perplexed and fairly overwhelmed, in the last light of what had surely been a very long day...

It was already dark when he found Hihvnor again, concluding an inspection and withdrawing to a point of observation somewhere near the middle of the lane that ran astride all the berths. He'd been rather difficult to spot in the gloom. There were a few torches out, but mostly the lights that would dot the city on any other night were unlit... no doubt as part of a universally understood effort to conserve lamp oil, like the SAPD had already set about doing. Besides that, Art spotted a few nav lights out in the Harbor a ways... nav lights on a large, frightful metal warship... one that was smartly lined up for a broadside barrage...

Just as he nearly reached Hihvnor, another Inquisition runner got there ahead of him...

"The foremen report all hands accounted for, Administrator," the runner informed him.

"Understood," Hihvnor replied. "Signal the *Temperance*." The runner dutifully leapt to his new order. "I am sorry to be so detained, Mr. Mallard," the Primary Administrator said then, as Art came up beside him. "Whatever remains on your mind, let us have it now, before the explosions start."

Art folded his arms – caught his breath – generally composed himself to be stern. He'd had a bit of time to think how he might put Hihvnor on the spot... and more than that, he'd resolved to give it a try...

"Alright," he began, "let's start with a recap. You won't take Rythigaar back to hold him liable behind your own bars. You won't execute him, like the state would do for most any broken rule... let alone the biggest one. And after all that, you go and tell me it's a *choice* to become an Inquisitor... a choice every one of you makes to swear off treasure. So answer me this one:

If he got to make that choice once, why not let him make it again? He regrets what he did, you know. He doesn't even have his treasure anymore... Horus said he dumped the whole thing on a countertop! Honestly, Hihvnor, if you really wish you could show him some amnesty, then I'd say do it. What are the odds he'll let you down again? And anyway, what are the *stakes*, even if he does?"

Hihvnor hung his head low. Even his coiled neck seemed to droop inside his vast hood. "You shame me, Mr. Mallard. Your words would seem to have wisdom and conviction, the likes of which cut deeper still, when they emanate from such an unlikely source."

"Thank you," Art put in.

"Even so, I am powerless. I cannot in and of myself defy a convention of 9000 years. The choice is made once... and *only* once. It is not for me alone to make allowances or excusals... or to offer second-chances. The Grand Inquisitors could, in theory, reexamine our policy. Unfortunately, it is not even within my power to appeal to them at present. Rythigaar is lost to us, and so he must remain, without remedy."

"Uh-huh," Art grunted. "Well, I suppose that pretty well sums-up your position. But that I call a *very* raw deal... for just a little old Human."

"Perhaps. And yet, perhaps you still do not grasp the full significance of the problem."

"Which problem is that?"

Hihvnor turned to regard him. "The problem of *greed*, my friend. The mode of the heart untrained against yearning. It is strongest and most gruesome in Avarica... I wouldn't hesitate to admit it. But it *is* a universal problem."

For a while, Hihvnor said no more... a bad habit of austere people, Art thought... to make you wonder what they meant, and to what extent. His eyes searched aimlessly into the harbor, maybe hoping to avoid deep introspection, while he tried to appear cool and indifferent. "Alright. Keep talking."

"You should consider this bit of work we are about to conclude here," Hihvnor invited him, looking over the shipyards. "It is not for nothing that we purge the excess of all peoples, the world over. Your Czarina is permitted certain extravagances, with regard to her station and her country's prosperity. But she is also a cautionary tale in her own right." He gestured out to the berths, each concealing some portion of a ship of incalculable value. "Look what she would have for herself, if we did nothing to moderate her. And yet, you can be sure, an entire harbor full of these ivory ships would not sate. The mind of greed is always set on the next trinket just beyond reach. The more it has, the more it craves, and all hindrance becomes insufferable. Your country has seen today how she reacts, when something goes unexpectedly against her – exacting punitive laws with childish abandon. And this is not the first time she has misbehaved. Our relationship with your Czarina has certainly been strained, at times. We foil her, as we must. But above all, we pity her. She has no idea how miserable she is."

A flare went up, temporarily casting the yards and the Inquisition battleship behind them with shocking bright light. Art watched as huge cannons made final adjustments...

"We're all dragons at heart, Mallard," Hihvnor went on. "We always hope for *more*, and then assuage ourselves that it is only natural. But more is never the answer. Those who want it must be denied. Those who persist must be made examples of. It is a hard way. But the other way is harder still."

With a series of earth-shattering sounds and brilliant flashes, the opening volley of the *Temperance* tore open the berths and concussed the very air roundabout, so that Art had to lean into the shockwaves, faltering and gasping for breath while his ears rung, and his eyes strained to focus. The crowds of Humans along the walk were every bit as visibly shaken. But the Inquisitors were unmoved.

Through the whole affecting show of zealous abolition, Art might have felt deeply validated in his reservations about the Inquisition. But, in the aftermath of the cannon fire, watching molten scaffolding crumble in on itself, dragging misbegotten dreams of the Czarina into shrieking, steaming depths, what he *really* felt was much more personal. In a way he never had before, Art felt doubt – doubt of the legitimacy of his own desires. And... in the midst of such doubt... he felt like he was watching his own dreams crumble, and fail in the reek...

...In the end, he would much rather have watched them sink his dumb fishing boat...

Chapter 8

If Horus had left Civil Headquarters slightly out-of-sorts, he was verging on downright surly by the time he reached the level of the train station. His errands had held him up, and he was bound to be late for the start of his office's evening circuit. After a while of goading himself to a jog – and even, for a brief while, a bit of a dignified run – his motivation escaped him. He reasoned that even at top speed for the duration, he'd arrive only just in time to watch the train start to creep away. Besides that, he was coming back empty-handed, making timeliness a moot point. So now, he merely trudged along, arms folded behind his back, reflecting grumpily.

There was a reason he'd taken to using a cab of late... and it didn't have to do with getting around town faster. Blucille Cordon made no idle prediction when she boded that the Mantid case would bring Horus fame, sans glory. In short, a lot of his interactions outside of court had soured of late. People were beginning to recognize him as that particularly contemptable defense lawyer who'd schemed, bamboozled, and obviously cheated his mass-murdering Mantid client out of a well-deserved state execution. The incidence of rude looks, terse conversations and '*hmphs*' on the street was steadily climbing. The folks at the bank had been especially unhelpful. The teller made a show of lethargically checking and double-checking Horus' subpoenas, vanishing to a back room for twenty minutes or so, and then coming back out only to inform Horus that the records he wanted had been shredded earlier that morning... along with all the other records. Horus had to admit under the present crisis that he couldn't tell if he was being duped or not. In the moment, it didn't seem to matter. By then he was already late and had no recourse but to take the teller at his word...

The journey through town afterwards only served to rub dirt in it... wading upstream through a sea of sour faces, each turning to avoid him... almost like he'd somehow become a scapegoat for the whole bewildering day. When he finally stopped to catch his breath at a street corner, he had his only passably friendly encounter on the whole walkabout. Wearing a reckless smile, the guy with the "Onyxadon is coming" sign gave him a reassuring pat on the shoulder. "You know..." the guy said, indicating his own sign, "...today's gonna seem like a walk in the park... when *he* shows up."

Generally, a day full of these kinds of interactions didn't weigh too heavily on Horus. He understood and accepted the lot of a Public Defender well enough. But today, he couldn't seem to shake examining it all through the lens of his old resolution... the one where he'd resolved never to do anything that might subject Deborah to the same kind of treatment...

He'd rationalized it like this: As long as she just worked for him, it couldn't very well be held against her. At any rate, it hadn't scuttled her popularity so far. But... if they were ever to become *more* than just coworkers... well, he hated to think of her getting the same sorts of ugly looks he fetched these days. And they were only bound to get worse, the more success he enjoyed in his work...

On the other hand, he wondered... what *did* he have to lose if he asked her out? She might just like the idea. She might just *go along* with it. And after all, he thought much too much of her to believe her shallow – the kind to choose being superficially celebrated by an adoring populace over a genuine, meaningful relationship. Nor was she naïve or helpless. Surely, he could trust her to make the choice for herself...

Of course, she could always say *no*. Yes, perhaps that was what he truly feared most. Not so much the rejection... but rather, carelessly destroying what they already had, all in a foolish gamble for something more. They got along so well, just as they were. He didn't know if he could bear to jeopardize it, surprising her with feelings she couldn't requite...

Horus groaned, catching himself in a familiar old mental vortex to nowhere. This was where all his present malaise had really started, anyway – his forced reexamination of his resolution, brought on by Art's rather careless meanderings on the subject of love. If Art had indeed found his own happiness, Horus was glad. But he ought to have the good humor not to try and drag everyone else along for the ride...

Finally, the station was in view. Horus was neither surprised nor unsurprised to see the train was still right where he left it after all. Likely enough, it would continue drilling in place until the economy started back up. But then again, maybe not. Who really knew?

His internal grumbling went on like that until at last he picked up his head to find the way up his own boarding stairs, only to see Deborah was at the top, leaning on the rail...

"What kept *you* all afternoon?" she asked smugly. "Or should I say, how did it go with Art's nails? Did you end up having to reattach any fingers?"

Horus grinned despite himself. Deborah was world-famous for her secretarial mastery, not her sarcasm... but he relied on both equally. She was – immediately – the cure for his dumpy attitude... even as she was also the cause...

"No amputations, I'm afraid," he answered. "The damage done was purely superficial."

She shrugged. "Just as well. Means I didn't miss anything."

He chuckled. "That you certainly didn't. Mostly, I was detained at the bank." He turned his empty hands up to her. "You see what I have to show for it."

"Oh dear," she frowned. "Was *that* the other errand you were going to run? But I already have all the bank statements we need..."

"You do? Well, that's some trick... if the bank tellers are to be believed."

She shook her head. "No trick at all. They were already in the file folders Blucille handed you this morning."

Horus clapped his hand over the top of his head. "Of course they were. Still, better to just be glad we have them. I don't know how we could hope to solve these fraud cases otherwise."

"These statements *would* seem to be the whole substance of the matter," Deborah agreed. "It all comes down to what we find tonight."

But Horus protested. "I think it will depend most on getting *paid* to look at them... whether we actually find anything or not."

She eyed him suspiciously. "Whatever you say, Boss."

* * *

A golden late afternoon gave way to a scarlet dusk, followed by a heavy darkness, filling in from the corners of the room, eating away the space of Horus' cozy little office car, while the two of them huddled together... reading off line after line of transactions...

"Deposit: seven pence and 49 shillings," Deborah recited from the bank statement.

"Mikael, personal check: seven pence and 49 shillings," Horus replied, reading off a photostat of the business' own ledger book. He set the sheet down with a crinkle. "Alright, any more entries?"

"Not on my sheet. You?"

"No."

"*Oo*kay," Deborah said doubtfully. "All the transactions match. Let's see how the final balances compare. I have three talents, one thousand four hundred twenty-five pence and 82 shillings. How about you?"

Horus begrudgingly returned the ledger to his face. "Three talents, one thousand *five hundred forty-two* pence and *12* shillings." He threw the dratted report away again. "Ten statements, ten books... each pair containing all the same transactions, in all the same amounts. And at the end... radically different final balances."

"In this case, a difference of 116 pence and 30 shillings," Deborah tallied.

Horus blinked. "That's some quick mental math."

Deborah examined her fingers coolly. "I've done time as a financial secretary, too, you know."

"I thought so," Horus replied, sighing. "In fact, I was counting on it to be more of a help."

"Well, the place to start would be to divide the difference in half. That's obviously the amount that got reported positive on the ledger, and negative on the bank statement. So we're looking at 58 pence and 15 shillings that got recorded wrong. Somehow."

"And yet, her charges add up to only 34 pence and 11 shillings," Horus asserted out of the blue.

Now, Deborah put her statement down. "Whose?"

"Vesta Djerkovic," Horus answered. "Her name's down for three transactions."

"I noticed her name, too. She's the financial expert the State got to check the books in your case."

"Not just in my case..." Horus boded. "In all *ten* cases."

Deborah's brow furrowed. "Oh really? No wonder you have her as a person of interest."

Horus nodded. "I've found it's best to entertain healthy suspicion wherever experts are concerned. But yes... all these similar cases, and the State has trusted only one set of eyes on the books. A set of eyes that, no less, belong to a patron on the same books..."

"*Some* of the books," Deborah cautioned, returning her eyes to the report.

"Yes," Horus admitted reluctantly. "There were some that didn't have her name at all. That also tends to frustrate my theory."

"Wait a minute," Deborah said, eyes bugged as she scanned more intently.

Horus' ears perked. "What is it?"

"Maybe there is something to this Vesta theory after all." She held out the statement, indicating an entry. "You read this one off as one of her payments. Look how it was recorded. Look *carefully*."

Horus took the sheet of paper and trained his eyes on her payment. "Four pence, two shillings," he read.

Deborah shook her head. "But did you see the *dash*?"

He looked at it again. "There *is* a dash in front of the amount. I thought it was just a speck in the paper, at first..."

"That's what I thought, too. Anyway, it's written up as a deposit. It's in *black*, not red. But if the dash is right..."

"...That would make the number *negative*," Horus completed her thought. He searched her eyes. "In all your days as a financial secretary, did you ever hear of a negative deposit?"

"No," Deborah admitted. "But that doesn't mean it isn't possible."

Horus stroked his jowls thoughtfully. "Alright. I think we're really onto something here. Something to implicate her. But the amounts are still wrong. We need to come up with 58 pence and 15 shillings. Moreover, we need a name that's on all ten of these ledgers. We need a *co-conspirator*."

"I need a snack," Deborah put in. "And a bit more light... especially if this all comes down to finding tiny little dashes. Doesn't it seem unusually dark tonight... or is it just me?"

"There's no light coming through the windows," Horus observed. They both got up, having silently resolved to investigate his rather strange discovery...

"No lamps out tonight," Deborah explained, once they'd spent a beat congregated there, in Horus' window... gazing on a suddenly alien landscape.

"I guess no one wants to spare the oil," he concluded.

Deborah shivered involuntarily. "It's downright eerie to look over the city like this. A city that never sleeps... all lights-out."

"Not entirely," Horus said, noticing something else... hesitating even to mention it. But of course, she would only find it on her own. "There's something aglow in the harbor." He swallowed. "Looks like a fire."

"*Fire*?" she repeated. "Where I come from, Horus, we call that a *blaze*. Looks like five ship lengths across... at least."

Without a thought, Horus threw open the window. Now, he could smell the smoke... hear the distant screams of police whistles in the streets. It was all rather visceral...

"Some day this turned out to be," he heard Deborah say, after an indeterminant time spent studying the world outside, from which he could learn nothing. He retracted his head through the window, finding her turned away, arms crossed. "A little bonkers, for my taste."

Horus gently closed his window. "I concur. First the economy... now some other nameless disaster..." He stopped himself, realizing he didn't really know what he was saying... watching her hang her head dejectedly. It was just like putting his heart in a vice, to see her in sudden doubt. Out of the two of them, she was always the resilient one. He needed to think of a way to snap her out of it. But with all his carefully trained intellect, he had no answer. Rationality seemed to fail in the face of so much confusion and chaos...

Finally, he just set a hand on her shoulder, and said what came from the heart...

"Tell me, Deborah... how do you believe two reasonable people ought to conduct themselves, in a world gone suddenly bonkers?"

She looked up at him, rallying a grin. "I suppose they just keep their heads. That way, when the dust settles, there's someone left to remind people what normal looks like."

Horus smiled, and nodded. "Sounds like wisdom to me." He crossed the room, rifling through his consumables. "Now, as I recall, we were about to get more light... and food."

* * *

A few candles and scrumptious morsels of moose-nose later, they were back in the zone, combing through the ledgers, refreshed and raring to catch a crook. But rather than carefully cross-reference the ledgers in the hopes of finding a name common to them all – a process that could generate numerous false positives (if they had many customers in common) as well as false negatives (if Vesta had multiple accomplices) – they realized it would be much smarter to simply hunt for more dashes...

"I found one," Horus said at last. "A *real* one this time, I'm sure." He had earlier thought he found one, only to look closer and see that it actually *was* just a speck in the paper. "Practically the very last entry for the month. Go figure."

"Okay," Deborah replied, holding out another ledger. "I found a couple in this one. But let's start with you. What name have you got?"

"'R. Atterboron'," Horus read aloud. "Personal check, paid on a charge account."

Deborah nodded. "Interesting."

Horus frowned. "*Interesting*? You mean, you have a different name?"

"Maybe and maybe not," she answered quizzically. "Mine is a personal check made out by a 'Rick'."

"*Rick...*" Horus repeated again. Something about the name struck him. He *knew* there was significance. He racked his brain to find it. The search took only a few very intense seconds...

"Yes, but of course it would be a Rick," he said. "Rick, as in, short for *Richard*. *Her* Richard, no doubt."

"Her deceased husband?"

Horus nodded. "Gone but not forgotten. And evidently, still writing checks."

"She'd be allowed to endorse them."

"Right," he said, checking his own ledger. "I'd bet the farm his full name is Richard Atterboron. Double or nothing, if we add the transactions under Vesta's own name with the 'Ricks' and the 'R. Atterborons', we'll solve the imbalances on all these statements."

Deborah smiled. "Let's find out!"

Thus began the rest of a long night of painstaking document review and simple math. Horus wouldn't have preferred to while it any other way. Certainly, he could not have wished for better company. Before long, the myriad cares and anxieties of the day – both personal and global, familiar and nameless – were forgotten. But he made a point of remembering one thing: his resolution. He felt downright silly now, for letting doubt over it get the better of him earlier...

Deborah and he *did* make an incredible team. And he was happy. *Very* happy... and confident of remaining so...

...Just as they were...

Chapter 9

Climbing back into town was a bit of an ordeal. Art definitely didn't want to be late, but he couldn't afford to exert himself very much, either – to show up at the station panting would simply lack decorum. It didn't help when he decided that this unexpected trip to the coast might've put him close enough to his 'secret sanctum' to swing by and change into an expensive sports jacket. Halfway there, he almost changed his mind about it, too... just paranoid enough to imagine he might be leading an Inquisitor tail straight to all his best stuff. But after a few clever double-backs, he put the idea to rest...

The pitstop slowed him up more than he'd hoped. He was forced to half-jog uphill for miles on what seemed an unusually warm, overcast night, all the while cursing himself for picking wool instead of cotton – lamenting that he could never seem to wear anything that wasn't either a 'jacket' or a 'coat' of some stripe or other.

And all that cloud cover ensured the night was not merely warm, but *dark*. The further he got into town – and the closer he got to the police station – the more this became a problem. The cops were out in force by this time, responding to the unexpected Inquisition raid on the royal shipyards. Following such a day of upheaval, the police department evidently felt a distinct need to ensure the people that the situation was under control. But of course, they didn't at that point have any way of knowing what the situation actually *was*... nor would they have had time to pause and explain it to everyone in the city anyway. Rather, what they needed was to pacify the commoners in the most condensed and efficient way possible. This resulted in their charging through the streets, blowing their whistles to get attention, and then shouting: "REMAIN CALM!" "THIS IS THE POLICE!" Or, perhaps the message was meant to be heard: "THIS IS THE POLICE!" "REMAIN CALM!" It didn't seem to matter much either way. If the escalating commotion among the night commuters wandering around in the dark was any indication, the department's assurances – while commendable – were far from effective. Before long, all manner of people were bumping into Art at a modest clip, Humans having even worse night vision than his own – and he, a black-furred fellow in a stygian sports jacket. Over time, this had the cumulative effect of something like wading through fisticuffs. Once, he was knocked clean off his feet. Moreover, it was his especially dubious fortune that an overloaded trashcan was right there on the corner to break his fall...

Through it all, however, he remained grateful of one thing: The landslide of new stressors served to bury those pesky misgivings that the visit to the Inquisition had stuck him with...

* * *

At last, the shambled form of Art Mallard arrived at the Civil Headquarters building, panting from heat and exhaustion. Standing in the light of the lamp over the front entrance (which they had fortunately decided to keep lit), he checked his pocket watch, and saw that he had at least managed to arrive fashionably late. His mind and nerves aflutter, he knocked on the front door, just as if he was picking her up at her house. He looked down and checked himself over. As he feared, the tumble over the trashcan had left him a mess... his expensive coat almost certainly ruined. *Oh well*... he'd just have to reason it away with suave witticisms...

Then he remembered the special little something he wanted to give her. He shot for his vest pocket... thankful to find it still there. But no time for relief... he realized his jowls were all foamy! He looked for a clean spot on his sleeve to wipe his face with. In the low light, he couldn't precisely make out what parts of his jacket were soiled; nothing seemed quite safe enough. But an idea occurred: Maybe he could stick his snout down the inside of his sleeve and wipe it off that way...

It was thus that Blucille had occasion to open the door to the police department building and find Art standing there with his nose up his shirt. With some pain and effort, he quickly freed his face, leaning with a hand against the inset wall, radiating posh sophistication...

"Hey there, Honey Bunch," he said, his whole body scalding while he forced himself to breathe slowly past his molten tongue. "What's shakin'?"

She looked him up and down with her lovely eyes, politely toning her initial expression of shock down to a cool bemusement. "There's been... some excitement," she said, unsure. "Some sort of trouble in the harbor." She squinted at him. "What's up with you? Are you ill? You smell like a bonfire..."

"Right as rain," he lied. "Never better."

Her eyes settled on his jacket. "What's that smeared all over your blazer?"

"I don't know," he answered. So much for suave witticisms...

She tapped a finger under her chin. "You know, we could always reschedule, if this is a bad time. I mean... what with the panic in the streets, and all..."

"Nah, it's fine," Art assured her with a wave of his hand.

Perhaps not so mysteriously, she remained a bit hesitant. But finally, she sighed her assent. "Oh, alright. I suppose Blackforest's order to behave frivolously still stands. Where are we going?"

Art beamed. "Why, only the swankiest joint in all of St. Argonsburg! Where else?"

"That doesn't bring any particular place to mind," she admitted.

"Just as well! Maybe you'll be pleasantly surprised yet!"

"That would be nice."

He turned and began to lead the way, with Blucille falling in-step. He would've really liked to offer her an arm, but the unidentified residue on his jacket obliged him to think better of it.

Shortly after starting off down the street, Blucille cleared her throat. "I noticed your nails. They look much better."

"Thanks," Art replied. "I think they turned out pretty well, all things considered..."

* * *

"So this is the swankiest joint in the whole city?" Blucille asked doubtfully, as they overlooked Rosie's Diner... a sleek, silvered composite of broken-down old train cars, given new life as a happening burger place.

"Swank is subjective," Art explained. "But I'm telling you, this place has got it going on! 1700 square feet of the loudest music, the greasiest food, the squooshiest benches and the slurpiest straws!"

"At least one of those things doesn't sound so bad. And it does appear to be open. But are you sure they'll actually serve us?"

"Sure I'm sure. Rosie owes me a favor. She thought her husband had gone and joined a digit cult. But I checked up on it, and it turned out to be just long hours at the office." He waved her on. "Come on! Time's a-wasting!"

* * *

After immediately excusing himself to the restroom to see what might be done about his ensemble – which didn't look too bad, after a few dozen passes of wet hand towels – Art gleefully plopped and scooted into the bench across from Blucille... truly, the very squooshiest. He leaned over the table, eager to commence the opening small-talk. But Blucille was sunk back into the bench, studying the wider restaurant, taking no apparent notice of his return.

"Nifty interior, eh?" Art said.

"It's certainly very chrome," she replied. "Not that I'm admiring it, per se. I was just checking for health code violations."

"Health code? What's that?"

"A great big heap of arbitrary bylaws for keeping food and food-service areas free of contamination."

He gave her a look. "But... why?"

She shrugged. "Humans are hypochondriacs, I guess. Either that, or their immune systems are terrible." She looked back at him. "Do we get a menu?"

"You won't need one," he answered energetically. "I've got just the thing in mind that'll knock your socks off." He looked down the aisle, reacting to a familiar grinding sound. "But look! Here comes the lady of the house with them now!"

Presently, a Human lady in a paper hat, a white-and-red skirt and matching roller skates came zooming up to their table. This was the Rosie of Rosie's Diner – both her and her business famous for the remarkable coincidence of sharing the same name. She looked stressed, but she managed a congenial smile, as soon as she recognized Art...

"Why, Art Mallard!" Rosie said. "So good to see you again! And you brought a lady-friend, I see!"

"Rosie, this is Blucille Cordon. Blucille, Rosie."

"Hello," Blucille replied.

Rosie handed Blucille a menu, but Art refused his. "You know I won't be needing that. I'll have the usual: a cherry soda and a Parasaurolophus burger swimming in fries and extra-extra au jus... no need to bother putting it on the grill... best vintage you've got. Oh, and uh..." he winked after nodding toward Blucille, "...make that a double order."

Rosie jotted all that down. "Sounds good. However, I hope you noted that house policy has changed. Until the economy is back up, I can take your orders, but I can't serve you any *actual* food."

Art was unphased. "Ah, come on, Rosie. Do it for me. We'll be all squared-up if you do."

Rosie's demeanor cracked a bit, Art's appeals really putting her on the spot. "Well... it's only store policy, and I am very grateful to know my husband's not a crazed heretic... but..."

"Do it, Rosie. Ms. Cordon here's an ADA. She promises not to press charges."

"But... I'm afraid it's not that simple, Mr. Mallard," Rosie confessed. "I literally *can't* make you raw burgers right now!"

Art blanched. "You can't?"

She shook her head. "We had a stock room full of meat that wouldn't keep while I can't sell it! So I did the only thing I could think of. We cured it all, Mr. Mallard. I've got nothing to serve you but jerky!"

Their collective hearts froze. *Jerky*, Art thought, knowing Blucille was privately lamenting the same. As he understood it, jerky was the heinous aftermath of some diabolical process by which you took all the tender, juicy, gamey character of meat and scorched it from existence... only to take whatever was left and go on cooking it for hours more...

"...I can still get you the cherry sodas," Rosie volunteered at length.

"Thanks, Sweetie," Art relented. "We'll take the sodas... and..." he couldn't keep the pain out of his voice as he arrived at the last word, "*...jerky.*"

Rosie kept looking on with concerned sympathy. "I'm really sorry. I know you guys like your food aged. If you want, I could pour you a bowl of stale Tasty Chunks cereal..."

"The jerky will be fine," Blucille said, and Art silently concurred.

Rosie nodded and went for the menu, but Blucille withheld it...

"I'd like to keep this a while anyway, if that's alright."

"Sure," Rosie said.

Art held out a hand to keep her there for one more line of questioning. "What about music, Rosie?" he asked. "I don't see your usual band." He turned to Blucille to explain. "They have this group of Meduseldan minstrels that performs here... they're a class act."

Rosie got that dino-in-the-headlights look again. "Goodness... I guess you didn't know..."

Art hesitated to ask. "Didn't know what?"

"Those guys all got conscripted to the Queens' War. They shipped out last week."

Art's ears folded back. "Well of all the rotten luck."

"We do have at least a temporary fill-in," Rosie assured him. "A local bard. I'll have him play some tunes for you. Only... cut him some slack. He's new to the job. Only knows one song, so far."

"Alright, Darlin'," Art replied with a grin, even as things continued to go against him. Rosie nodded one last time before sadly skating away...

"So what about these 'cherry sodas'?" Blucille asked. "I've never heard of it..."

Art perked up a tad. "It's this crazy new thing they do... you get a really sugary drink and blast a bunch of carbon bubbles in it."

Her brow furrowed. "Whose idea was that?"

He shrugged. "Some old dead grape juice peddler, I'm told. Word is, he came up with it as a last-ditch idea to save his vineyard. To his own surprise, it actually took like wildfire! Only then, all the bigger vineyards just copied him and ran him out of business anyway."

Blucille sighed. "Well, that's life, isn't it?"

Art's grin flattened. "Yeah. Kinda."

* * *

The next twenty minutes failed to improve the overall trajectory of the evening. Even though the entrée was already long done – and well in abundance of anything the two of them might have liked – still Rosie kept them waiting on it, if only to give them the full benefit of the sit-down restaurant experience.

Now, if Art had only kept his big mouth shut about the music, it was at least conceivable that Blucille and he might have spent this time engaged in pleasant chit-chat. Then again, a spot of dancing to hip tunes would have been even better. But neither was to be his good fortune... and indeed, far from it. The 'bard', as he feared, turned out to be a Human... and not one possessed of much promise. Not that Humans were especially poor musicians, necessarily... but they suffered from the curious and very unfortunate tendency to perform Human *songs*...

That Rosie had initially enlisted the talents of Meduseldan minstrels was one of the things that really set her place apart. Meduselda were the *real* masters of music, having invented it in the first place. And while they weren't very experiential creatures by nature, they managed well enough to imbue their songs with rich history, which they'd seen more of than any other species. A Meduseldan ballad could effectively transport you through time to an era you'd never even heard about. But *Human* songs... they were, to a one, substanceless affairs – mostly a lot of bawling of various intransitive interjections, such as, "Whoa," "Yeah," "Hey," or, "Tonight." Coincidentally, this bard's go-to song just so happened to be a chart-topper in the contemporary Human genre, whose dynasty had plagued the wider musical world for seemingly the last century, and whose title was – appropriately enough – "Whoa, Yeah, Hey, Tonight." Equally appropriate, the 'lyrics' of the song went something like, "Whoa, Yeah, Hey, Tonight..." over and over, ad nauseum. If, perchance, the song also happened to contain any actual words, Art had so far managed not to note their presence...

After they managed to survive the initial performance, Art knew a beat of momentary reprieve, remembering vaguely back in the folds of time to when Rosie had said that the bard only knew one song. This, however, was apparently not enough to stop the young man trying to put on a whole show. Just about as Art was beginning to make a witty remark about the final end of their ordeal, the bard launched immediately into an encore...

The racket had already proven prohibitive of any conversation. And *dancing*? Unthinkable... even to save their lives. Art ended up spending the whole second and third performance staring at the back of Blucille's menu, while he tried to dream up a polite way to cover his ears...

The one silver lining in all this was that the cherry sodas were still top-notch. They both went through something like four of them. But this went on to ensure that when the noise finally relented, the problem of fluid retention arose just in time to mitigate their relief.

Then at last, when Art felt he could hold it no longer, the food showed up...

"Hm," Art concluded, now thoroughly convinced that the second bite was even worse than the first. "Well, I don't know about you, but this is a meal I'll remember."

He watched Blucille study the stick of jerky in her hand while a wide assortment of pained expressions modulated across her slowly-chewing face. "I think it might be better if it was... if it was..."

"Yup," Art agreed. "That *would* be an improvement."

She wrapped her snout in her napkin for what seemed a long time to be merely wiping her face. When she'd set it aside, he couldn't help wondering if her bite of jerky was bound up in it somewhere. Then she went to slurp the taste out of her mouth with the fifth soda...

Art sighed. There was no denying he'd reached *that point*... the point that every gentleman dreaded, where the date had gone so insufferably bad that the only thing left to do was admit it... and, in so doing, throw himself at the mercy of the lady, begging a raincheck...

"Listen, Blucille," he began, after a pass of his own napkin. "I know this whole thing's been a wash. But I hope you'll let me make it up to you some other day. I really wanted to show you a good time." There. He'd demonstrated his sincere soft side. Now what he needed was a confident chaser. He cleared his throat, drawing himself up very straight. "Anyway, now we've tried my lousy idea. So answer me this one: What does Blucille Cordon enjoy doing outside of work?"

She looked at him, then... and it wasn't at all the look he'd hoped to see. Her eyes were sharp... stern... perhaps even a little sad...

"Outside of work? Is that a rhetorical question?"

Art thoughtlessly tugged at his collar. "Well... no," he answered weakly. "I mean, of course not. There must be *something* you like to do. Name it, and we'll do it. It could be anything. Anything at all..."

He nearly trailed off before he stopped himself. The way she looked at him belied his every appeal. He was left to sit there incredulous. Somehow, he'd *wounded* her, just trying to be nice...

"I do what I have to... as much as I can handle," she answered him at length. "And that's all there is." Her voice was hollow, and it left him feeling very much the same...

After she'd plunged him in icy despair a few moments longer, her face turned up with a sarcastic grin as she shot for her purse... if only to busy herself rustling its contents. "Anyway, I don't know why you insist on a silly question like that when you already know the answer."

He winced. "What do you mean?"

"Oh come now, Mr. Mallard, don't try to plead ignorance," she laughed mirthlessly, retrieving her pipe. "It doesn't suit you."

Now, he began to feel hurt himself – indignant. "Blucille, I honestly have no idea what you're on about."

"Don't you? Am I really expected to believe that you don't already know everything there is to know about me? *You* – a professional snoop – and I, a public servant. No doubt my whole life is an open book to *you*. Now you're going to sit there and tell me you haven't been reading up?"

He threw up his hands. "On my word, I haven't!"

"Well, what in creation is all this about, then?"

"What's *what* about?"

"*This*!" She gestured widely. "*All* this. The ridiculous pet names – the masterfully played part of the endearing oaf – all those things he used..." She cut herself off, regressing from virtual outrage back into a smug sneer. Then she blew a strand of bubbles. "Well, there I go again. Trying to buy into the delusion – explaining things you already know full-well. What else could account for your interest? My spunk? My charming personality? *Please*. It could only be that you found out all about *Blucille Cordon*." Her voice took on a subdued mocking tone, while she proceeded to put words in his mouth. "Poor, sad, damaged Blucille. She must be so lonely... so tragically, *conveniently* vulnerable. She wouldn't turn away a hunk like me. She couldn't afford to."

At first, Art made no sign. But finally, with a slow exhalation, he took the napkin down from around his neck. And he stood to go...

"It's been a long day," he said. "Much too long for a moment more of this. I don't know a thing about your past, Blucille. Not a *darned* thing. And I don't really know what it is I see in you. Right now it's especially unclear. But I for one thought there was more to life than work... or anyway, I held out hope there was, before today. And for some dumb reason I got the idea that you might be a swell gal to share it with. I guess that makes me a sap."

He began to walk away. But before he made it more than a few steps, he *remembered*. He remembered about the silly little token he'd picked up on the roadside. He took the thing out of his pocket and tumbled it around. And then, without coherent reason – even though he certainly should have let the matter rest – he returned with it...

"One more thing," he said, extending his hand. "Take this."

She turned and searched him – alternating lancing looks at the present – puzzled and upset. "What is it?"

"It's lavender," he answered. "I found it growing by the street. I never knew it looked like these silly little purple stemmy things, but I recognized the scent."

She went blank. "Why are you giving it to *me*?"

"I know how much you like the smell. You always use lavender soap for your pipe. Sorry to notice something about you. But I guess you were right. I turned out to be a snoop, after all..."

He left the sprig on the table in front of her, then quietly blustered out of Rosie's Diner. He managed not to notice her start to call after him... nor could he have guessed the regret he left her saddled with. It was all lost on him as he stepped back into the darkness, while his mind decided to further compound his torment by recalling the speech Hihvnor gave him at the shipyards. It would have been enough for him, just to get past that disastrous night. But on top of that, he was left to wonder if he'd only got exactly what he had coming to him...

...Just for hoping...

...Hoping for *more*...

Chapter 10

Horus groaned, extracting himself from his desk. His jowls hung heavy from his snout as he rubbed an impressive layer of crust out of his eyes. He turned blinking to face the dazzling light coming through his window, the fog in his brain slowly abating. He searched space aimlessly for several seconds while the prior day's events presented themselves for sorting. He had a time of it, trying to distinguish the facts from some bizarre dream he may have had. Surely, he thought, his unconscious mind must have contrived *some* of it. But no. Yesterday had seen a legal end to the economy, an unexplained fire in the harbor, a jailbird Inquisitor, and any of a number of other abnormalities, ranging from the merely curious to the downright disturbing. Still – somehow – in the light of a new day, even the bedrock facts of life that remained in doubt seemed trifling. He stretched, he shook, and he rose... ready to pick right back up, wherever real life had left off...

Whether or not he perceived it, the majority of St. Argonsburg was currently experiencing the same sense of waking up from a fever-dream. Though nothing had expressly changed, and money was still illegal, the fear-induced, tight-fisted conservancy of the day before had virtually vanished overnight. The unspoken new consensus was that – money or no – it was much easier to continue doing your job if, in the process, you were actually still providing other people with your goods and services. Anyway, most folks knew somebody who had already spent the previous day conducting pro-bono business as usual, without apparent arrest or execution...

In the course of the morning, Horus was to note that one of the few people not greatly refreshed was Art Mallard. The PI slumped his way through a detailed report of his visit to the Inquisition Outpost, and said little else. Horus didn't dare ask how the date went: The answer was glaring. Of course, they would have to talk about it eventually. But maybe right now just wasn't the best time...

After all, there was work to do. He knew now with certainty what the Inquisition planned to do about Rythigaar... which was to say, *nothing*. This stance and the reasoning for it had to be relayed back to Hamilton Blackforest, as agreed. Moreover, he needed to stay apprised of what the DA himself planned to do with his client... a much more nebulous situation. He hoped Hamilton would have got word from the justice department by now, instructing him what to do with suspects held over for illegal use of money. But even if nothing there had so far changed, he needed more time to confer with his client. He needed to pick up his copy of Rythigaar's written statement... and perhaps use it to pursue an interesting new avenue of investigation...

...And, finally, he meant to enlist the help of the department, in perpetrating a ruse...

In any case, all roads led him back to the Civil Headquarters building...

* * *

Just as he was finishing his check-in at the front desk, Horus noticed a familiar face coming his way... a fixture of the department, really, whose apparent absence the day before suddenly struck him curious. It may have had something to do with the fact that, today, he was advancing at a shamble, looking drained and pasty. And, if that was not enough, he was currently walking abreast one of Horus' other, more nightmarish acquaintances...

"Ah, Milo," Horus called. "Good morning." He immediately regretted the greeting, since it was patently obvious that this was *not* Deputy Constable Miloje's idea of a good morning. But, formalities being what they were, he couldn't very well help it.

"Templar," Miloje called back, concluding his own formalities. "If I can be any help to you at all, you will have to keep it brief."

"Keep it down!" Doctor Nokkaeru commanded him. "All your noise is clouding the data."

Horus had no immediate context for the doctor's outburst, but after a cursory study of the situation, he noticed that there was some tube protruding from beneath the shirt of Miloje's uniform. It ran up, down, over, and into a forked caliper-like apparatus clamped over Nokkaeru's mask, about where her earholes would be. Horus was as curious as he was privately amused. He knew the Deputy Constable deplored the company of their resident Plague Doctor, much as Horus himself did. But presently, she was not just following him around... she was apparently attached to him...

"And good morning to you, Dr. Nokkaeru," Horus grudgingly acknowledged her.

"Don't distract me with your pleasantries, Councilor," she replied. "Even were this the day of your disaster, my attention is needed elsewhere."

"My... a bit brusque today, are we?" Horus goaded, gladly returning his attention to Miloje. "Both of you. I thought sure the next time I saw you, I'd get some witty remark about turning your department's lobby into a day spa, straight off. Surely you heard about that..."

"I did," Miloje said as he arrived in front of Horus, looking thoroughly displeased, if not pained. "But I've been advised to refrain from gratuitous sarcasm for the time being." His eyes shifted icily toward the Heron next to him. "It allegedly has an adverse effect on my blood pressure."

Horus' amusement was finally tempered with a bit of sober sympathy. "I'm sorry, Milo. You do seem... rather ill."

There was a fresh spark in Miloje's eye, then. "Oh, yes? I wonder what gave me away. Was it my general pallor? Or, perhaps the fact that I am literally *tethered* to a health care professional provided some clue?"

"Really, Deputy Constable," Nokkaeru cautioned. "Your blood pressure."

"Of course," Miloje replied, mustache twitching. "Now, Templar, as I said, please do get right at the point. What do you need here?"

"A number of things, I'm afraid," Horus admitted.

"*Naturally,*" Miloje grunted. "What is of *principle* importance, then?"

"I suppose, I should talk with Hamilton first."

Miloje shook his head. "He is currently indisposed. Sorry."

"Really? Is the whole department coming down with something?"

"We've had quite a lot on our plate, the last twenty-one hours. First the new law, and then a most unexpected scuttling of our royal shipyards last night, at the hands of the Inquisition. Blackforest hasn't quite recovered from that episode. Mostly, he's occupied himself thus far today by staring at his desk, and chanting to himself, 'No one tells me anything'."

Horus blinked. "Well, he'll certainly have to snap out of it sooner or later. I have a client moldering in the jail, waiting to learn just when and how he'll be charged."

"I can relay some news on that front. We are expecting a decree to come down from the Czarina's office by the stroke of eleven, rescinding the one from yesterday, and reinstating the economy."

Horus twinged with surprise. "Well, that's unexpected. I'd thought she would hold out longer than a mere day..."

Miloje shrugged. "Perhaps the sudden loss of a small fleet softened her. Who knows? But the order is coming."

"What does that mean for my client, precisely?" Horus pressed him. "He still broke the law... while it *was* a law."

Miloje declined to answer, instead looking past Horus, down another wing of the department building. "Ah, there now: someone else who can answer your questions."

Horus followed his gaze and found Captain Alexei approaching from behind him...

"...But there is one other thing you neglected to mention, Templar," Miloje went on. As Horus turned back to face him, he found the Deputy Constable holding out a rolled-up document. "You asked for this, didn't you? I was told to proffer it, or else stick it in the mail, if you failed to appear before midday."

Horus took the papers and promptly identified them. "Rythigaar's statement," he declared. "Thank you, Milo... I'll have to see what kind of use I can put this to."

Miloje raised a brow. "I suppose you intend to enlist the analysis of our new graphologist?"

Horus shrugged. "This seems as good an opportunity as any to find out whether he might be a worthwhile resource."

Miloje only waved it off. "If pseudoscience is your flair, far be it from me to discourage you."

"*Ahem*," the doctor cut in.

"Right," Miloje said, rolling his eyes. "I must be off, Templar. No one so endangers me to engage in sarcasm as you do. But here, let Captain Alexei help you." He tipped his hat to leave. "Good day."

"Good day, Milo," Horus nodded. Then, he nodded to the doctor, too. "Dr. Nokkaeru." She barely nodded back.

* * *

"I want to thank you again for clearing my name, Mr. Templar," Captain Alexei said, as he escorted Horus back to the holding cells. "I'm most grateful to you... as I am to the Creators that the lad wasn't killed. I should never have lived with a dead Inquisitor on my conscience."

Horus chuckled. "You'll have to stop thanking me eventually, as I actually did nothing for you. But if you insist on feeling indebted, a few answers will more than suffice to pay me back. Do you know what's to become of Rythigaar? Has it been determined yet that illegal use of money is a capital offense?"

The Captain blanched. "Why, no... it hasn't. I'm afraid there is still no prescribed punishment for illegal use of money. Now that the law has been rescinded, in fact... there likely never will be."

Horus stopped in his tracks. "Never?"

Alexei shrugged his most apologetic. "It's a bear of a situation, Sir. The justice department is mired with nearly as many suits as the country has people. The banks destroyed all their financial records, fearing they would be deemed illicit goods. Now they are suing the Clerical Dronehood of Berlberi for records they archived. But the Dronehood is loath to turn them over. It is their position that if the banks destroyed a great wealth of paperwork, they're liable to commit such an atrocity again."

Horus' head swam. Hardly could more nonsense be condensed into just a few sentences. He had a hard time deciding what to ask first. "Why would the banks sue for each citizen's records, independently? Why not file a class-action suit?"

Alexei shook his head. "I couldn't hope to speculate, except to say that the banks seem to have a flair for the dramatic these days. And now, the Dronehood, the courts, and everyone in the country is going to pay for their grandstanding. We're *all* likely to be audited for the last few months, so that the banks can restore their records to the present day."

Another doubt struck Horus suddenly. "Goodness... what about current account *balances*? What are we all going to do if the banks have no present idea how much money we have?"

"Oh, there's no trouble there, Sir," Alexei assured him. "Every account box still contains the proper amount... up to the last permitted transaction."

Horus' brow knit together. "*Contains* the amount? As in, in hard cash?"

He nodded. "Yes, Sir. Does that surprise you?"

"More than a little. That would seem to mean an awful lot of coin-jockeying on any given day."

Alexei shrugged. "It has the virtue of security, and it keeps the bankers busy."

Horus endeavored to shake away all his superfluous questions and refocus on Rythigaar's plight. "Well, never mind. You were explaining about the courts... why they haven't arrived at a punishment for illegal use of money yet..."

"Ah yes. As I say, they are quite bogged-down with the bank suits. They are working to reclassify them... to consolidate them. But it will take time.

And while they're busy sorting that out, it's most unlikely they'll bother arbitrating a punishment for your client's crime."

Horus wondered at the Captain's word choice. "My *client's* crime? You say that almost as if he's the only offender."

"That's because he *is*, Mr. Templar. The *only* one."

Horus was a bit incredulous. "Really? In the entire country?"

Alexei nodded. "Likely there were other incidents, but it seems they weren't reported."

Horus sighed. "And I'm sure the courts know that the *only* accused is an Inquisitor. No doubt they were hoping, as Hamilton has been, that the Inquisition would handle this matter themselves. That *Hamilton*..." Horus reflected, half-cursing. "He's shut up in his office right now, when he ought to be putting pressure on the courts to reach an arbitration. That's his *job*: to facilitate convictions..."

"Mr. Blackforest maintains there's nothing he can do," Alexei lamented.

"Nothing he's *willing* to do, anyway," Horus corrected. "He's been dratting all this confusion, but he's just wily enough to turn it to his advantage. He made it quite clear yesterday that he doesn't want to touch this Inquisitor thing with a forty-foot pole. So he'll go right on feigning his hands are tied." Horus scratched under his chin, taking mental stock. Merely pointing the finger at Hamilton would get nowhere. He needed to reassess things...

"Alright," Horus went on to say, essentially thinking out loud. "We've established that the Inquisition won't take Rythigaar back to punish him..."

"Is that quite certain?" Alexei leapt in to ask.

"Yes. And we've also established that the courts won't bind him over to trial, because there is no prescribed punishment for the law he broke, which is no longer a law." He looked at Alexei. "So, see if you can answer me this, Captain: If no one would hold Rythigaar liable... why not simply let him go? Or, maybe more to the point: What grounds do you even have for holding him any longer?"

Alexei fidgeted quite uncomfortably, as Horus put him on the spot. "Well, of course, that *sounds like* a fair question, Sir. But here again, we're in uncharted waters. We've never once released anyone who was not first tried and then acquitted. Legally, we can't."

Horus planted his head in his palm, letting his hand fall slowly down his snout. "Yesterday, I reminded the District Attorney that the last thing a Public Defender should ever do would be to encourage someone to pursue charges against his client. And yet, from what you're telling me, that seems to be the *only way* I can possibly hope to help him."

"I'm not sure I follow, Sir," Alexei muttered.

"Then let's remove all doubt," Horus replied. "Unless I can first get my client into court, there's no way he can be released? He'll simply be put up in a cell for the rest of his life, neither innocent nor guilty?"

Alexei nodded solemnly. "Yes. If, as you claim, the Inquisition should never come to round him up, I'm afraid that is just what will happen."

Horus sighed, his shoulders in a slump. "And here I thought today was going to be more normal."

"I am very sorry, Mr. Templar," Alexei assuaged him. "You should know I would have preferred to give you better answers. I feel more in your debt now than when we started."

Horus patted him on the shoulder. "It's quite alright, Alexei. None of this is your fault. Or anyway, not very much of it." He had a thought, then... another matter the Captain might help him with. "Yet maybe there's something else you can clarify for me." He looked furtively up and down the corridor. "You may decline to answer; it's not really any of my business. But... do you know what's wrong with the Deputy Constable?"

"Not precisely," Alexei admitted. "I know he took rather ill yesterday... it seems he over-exerted himself when we gave chase to your client. Doctor Nokkaeru is presently testing him for something outside our native understanding of medicine. I believe she called it... heart arrhythmia?"

"*Heart arrhythmia...*" Horus repeated. "It sounds serious."

"It is... if in fact he has it. Apparently, the only way to be sure is for her to follow him everywhere, listening to his heart night and day." He became sullen again. "Truthfully, I'm not sure what to hope for, Sir. The Herons can diagnose it, but even *they* can't treat it. But on the other hand, even if he comes back negative, that will only mean the attack he suffered yesterday remains a mystery – one that the best medicine available cannot solve."

"Well, so much for cheering you," Horus lamented. "But I thank you for the answers... and I join you in hoping for the best." He looked down the hall. "Anyway, I suppose it's time to be moving on. Good, bad, or no news at all, I still owe my client a visit..."

* * *

"So, that's the long and short of where we stand," Horus said, seated across from Rythigaar, who was chained to the big, sturdy table between them. "I wish I could say where we go from here. But honestly, at present, I can't think of a way to maneuver."

"That is no grief to me, Mr. Templar," Rythigaar replied. "I can see you're doing your best, as every man should."

"And I'll continue to," Horus assured him. "You have my word."

An interval of silence passed. Horus studied his client – a day out from traumatic surgery, and already sitting tall, straight and unflinching. He had some of the bearing of an Avarican, it seemed. That he had spent years in their company – and indeed, had probably been raised by them – was clear. Bereft of any other present inspiration, Horus found himself wanting to know more about Rythigaar. He'd seen it many times before: If he only asked enough questions, something enlightening always came up...

"Why don't you tell me a bit about yourself, Rythigaar?"

The man hesitated. "Myself?"

"Yes," Horus grinned. "It occurs to me: I really don't know anything about you at all."

"You know my former occupation," Rythigaar argued. "You know my crime. I can't imagine what else would be pertinent..."

"You let me be the judge of that. Come now, you wrote up an entire dissertation here about your trespass," Horus said, showing his copy of the statement. "Surely you can afford to volunteer a few more details."

Rythigaar's mask trained down to the table as he peered back into his catalogue of memories. "I once set a thumb tack on my instructor's chair. I was seven years old at the time... plenty old enough to know better. Ironically, the instructor didn't even notice the tack when he sat on it. I was forced to tell him later and point it out, when my conscience at last got the better of me. At age nine, I misunderstood the safety mechanism when I was first being drilled with a snail pistol. I misfired. Fortunately, no injuries resulted. At age thirteen, I fell behind in my studies and skipped several volumes of Magormissahr's *Ref*..."

"...Just a moment," Horus interrupted, hand extended. "Perhaps I mischaracterized my question by bringing up your written confession. I was looking for general things about *you*, yourself... not just a list of your wrongdoings."

"I'm unsure of the distinction," Rythigaar admitted.

Horus crossed his arms. “Alright. Why don’t we start with the elephant in the room. You’re a Human Inquisitor. That’s unusual. Would you tell me how that came to be?”

Rythigaar sighed. “It’s a formulaic tale, at best. I was orphaned nearly at birth. My parents both died in a tragic crocheting accident. There were no next-of-kin to raise me. The Inquisition often steps in, in such cases.”

“I suppose I should have known you spent your whole life in their care,” Horus said. “What with a name like ‘Rythigaar’.”

He nodded. “It is distinctly Avarican.”

“Tell me about your adoptive parents,” Horus suggested. The question seemed to cause Rythigaar unexpected consternation...

“They were good stern folk, who graciously offered to raise me alongside their two hatchlings,” he answered at length. “It was my good fortune to grow up knowing several generations of both sides of my family.” He paused again. “Really, Mr. Templar, I don’t greatly relish visiting this subject. My family will know my betrayal by now. I hate to think what I’ve put them through. They’ve already endured so much disgrace...”

Horus frowned. “I’m sorry. Much as I try, I don’t seem able to steer things very far from your guilt.”

He shrugged. “It can’t be helped. And it shouldn’t. For me there is nothing else.”

Horus deeply wished to object... but he could find no grounds. The Inquisition accounted for Rythigaar’s whole life. And now, irrevocably, he’d lost it. How could a man be comforted, feeling he’d thrown *everything* away? But while he agonized over the question, Rythigaar continued...

“If you don’t mind my inquiring of you again, Councilor,” he started, “do you think that, perhaps, you ought to reconsider your own position here? It seems to me you’ve investigated my case quite thoroughly. And, whether you wish to accept it or not, you’ve arrived at a conclusion: I am to be left here, in this jail. I have no qualms with that. It is fitting. In fact, I’d go so far as to say I’d be *grateful*, if you would simply let things lie.”

Horus shook his head. “Don’t you do that, Rythigaar. I can’t entertain any more indifference about your future. The SAPD wants to leave you here. The Inquisition wants to leave you here. I won’t accept *you* wanting to leave *yourself* here. A Public Defender can only take so much.”

“But it *is* my wish,” Rythigaar contended. “And you’re tasked with representing my interests.”

Horus tried to stare him down. He gave him a very piercing look... one that could crack the common witness. But it was useless. He couldn't match gazes with an Inquisitor – couldn't penetrate that featureless mask, or unsteady that unflinching countenance. Finally, he relented the attempt. He stood to go...

"Very well," he seemed to give in, at first. "So help me, I'll leave you here too... if it comes to it. But while you're pent up, and you have nothing else to think about beside your sins, consider this: Whether or not *you* wish to accept it, you've been given a very extraordinary gift. You have a second chance. You erred the greatest way you knew how, and yet, your life goes on. In this country, that's unheard of. And I don't think it's the kind of thing that ought to go to waste."

Rythigaar turned his shackled hands up. "But even if I were released, where would I go? And what would I do?"

Horus sighed. "I don't know. But suppose I think of something. And suppose I can find a way to arrange for your release. Would you go? Would you make something of your second chance?"

Rythigaar nodded deeply. "Yes, Mr. Templar. You may be certain I would."

Horus smiled. "Good. That's a start I can work with..."

Chapter 11

Horus knocked on the door. It was a simple act, but it took a bit of winding himself up to do. This was, unquestionably, the door he'd been looking for. But he'd hardly expected to find it in a disused corner of the Civil Headquarters' basement, between a pair of broom closets. It was a most unusual place for a monogramed door of mirrored glass. But then, the SAPD had never really expected to accommodate a house graphologist. Nor did Horus suppose they were in much hurry to avail themselves of his expertise, if Miloje's pseudoscience comment was any clue. Admittedly, the whole idea of graphology *was* a bit on the fringes. That one could, by careful analysis of a subject's handwriting, unearth hidden truths about their persona was, at best, a colorful notion. Horus himself was skeptical to say the least. He went down there knowing full-well he might have to grin and bear through the meaningless balderdash of a crackpot for the next hour. Standing now in the dark underbelly of the department building, smelling old mops, he was not greatly encouraged...

Nor could he shake a nagging unease, as he studied the hastily-applied, runny monograms on the door...

Milt Lias Creevey, PhD. – Graphology

He jumped ever so slightly when that door suddenly came open...

"Well, hello!" a big, healthy Human with keen eyes and a genuine smile greeted him. "Don't tell me – you must be Horus Templar. I'm Dr. Creevey... but please, call me Lias. Middle names are expensive, you know, so I like to get mileage out of it."

Horus found himself already in the midst of a handshake so flawlessly executed that he couldn't even remember the initiation. Dr. Creevey's grip was equally ideal... neither insincerely noodly nor some sort of macho hand-crushing contest – a perfect equilibrium of authenticity. And, most astonishingly, they both decided the handshake was over at *precisely* the same instant. Horus was honestly a bit bewildered by all this charisma, perhaps only just realizing how much he'd truly been expecting an eccentric half-wit. To find someone so obviously bright and personable instead was a bit much...

...*Almost* too *much*, Horus thought...

...But then, maybe it was just the goatee...

"Pleased to meet you, Lias," Horus replied, putting on his own best authentic air. "I apologize for coming down here without so much as an appointment."

"No trouble at all!" Lias laughed it off. "I'm not exactly up to my eyeballs in work down here, Mr. Templar. I've been here nearly three weeks, and in that time, how many lawmen do you think have come to my door, begging my analysis?"

Horus grinned a bit nervously. "I hope you won't think me rude if I guess none."

Lias shook his head. "No, not rude... just a good guesser." He gestured at his desk. "Come now! Have a seat."

As they took chairs opposite one another, Lias plopped down with an informal ease, harsh rays from a small cellar window near the ceiling lancing down on his shoulders. "Truthfully, Horus..." he stopped himself. "May I call you Horus?"

"You may."

"Well, Horus... I can honestly say I didn't think I'd be meeting you, personally."

Horus just smiled impassively. Never mind, he still had no idea how Dr. Creevey even knew who he was. "No?" he asked simply.

"Not especially. I figured, if you had any mind at all to consult me, you'd probably do it by proxy. What's your detective friend's name again?" He snapped his fingers as he deliberated. "Artimus Mallard!"

"That's right," Horus nodded, adding to his list of people he was surprised Lias already knew about. "And on an ordinary day, you might've been correct. But I thought this time I'd spare Art the trouble. I already had other business here at the station." Horus went on, though he couldn't be sure why. "...And, it seemed like he could use a day off."

Lias had a sympathetic look. "His date with Blucille Cordon must've gone South, then?" He sighed. "It's a shame. That Blucille's had a pretty hard go of it, you know. I'm sorry for them both."

Horus could feel his ear twitch. "For someone who's been retained less than half a month, you certainly seem to know who's who, and what's what. Maybe better than I do."

Lias waved it off boisterously. "Well, like I say, official business has been slow... but a man's gotta keep busy." He grabbed a bunch of papers off his desk, holding them up. "I stay pretty well in practice, just pouring over old forms. I've learned quite a lot about the SAPD, and its contacts. Quite an awful lot."

As he let the papers slide back onto the desk, Horus took a closer look at them. They really *were* just old forms... internal office documents, mostly with a lot of check boxes... at best, a short essay field, here and there...

"I see," he said, still trying to sound impassive, rather than a little creeped-out. "You're plying your graphology on your own coworkers?"

He shrugged dramatically. "No documents in there I'm not allowed to look at... *honest*. And anyway, like I say, it's good practice."

Horus leaned over the desk, folded his hands... maybe unconsciously turning this into a bit of a cross-examination. "You must be quite proficient, to learn from these forms of my detective's date last night. He only set it up yesterday afternoon."

Lias chuckled. "Well, you learn some from the water cooler, too." He clapped his big strong hands. "But now: What is it you came to see me about, Horus? I'm only too eager to help."

Horus nodded, and produced Rythigaar's written statement. "I'd be obliged if you'd analyze this for me. My latest client is a retentive one. I can't seem to draw much out of him without a lot of unnecessary pain. So this seemed an ideal opportunity to test your mettle."

"To see if I peddle a lot of hogwash, I suppose you mean." He took the statement, giving it an opening scan.

"That's a more... *indelicate* way of putting it," Horus admitted.

"People's skepticism doesn't bother me, Horus," Lias said, taking out a jeweler's loupe. "I enjoy poking big fat holes in it." He started a very careful, very close examination. "Interesting fellow, this client of yours," he said. "Very shy around the ladies... likes the color green... suffered horrible acne in his teen years."

"Any sign of a crushing existential guilt complex, by chance?" Horus asked.

Lias looked up at him, puzzled. "Not really. Where do you think I'd get that from?"

Horus blinked. He'd read every word of the statement prior to this meeting... and if there was one overriding theme, it was guilt. "Evidently, your analysis doesn't concern trifles like the actual *content* of the writing."

"Nah," Lias waved it off. "Any literate person can look at this and read the lines. Graphology's mostly reading *between* them."

Horus was, for a moment, deeply unsettled. "Let's clarify an important point here: You're not suggesting my client wrote this confession *without* genuine remorse?" He reeled at the very thought. "If you are, I'll be very beside myself..."

"That's not what I'm saying," Lias answered. "The words he used... the thoughts and feelings behind them... that's all surface stuff. I don't see any of that... I look right past it. I see the things he *wasn't* writing about, but were too important not to get mixed up in there anyway."

Horus sighed his relief. "Well, I'm glad to have that settled. I would hate to think all the piety was just an act."

"Nope," he said, returning to his analysis. "Your client's an honest one, I can see that. And devout. But even the honest ones have layers to peel back. Sometimes *especially* the honest ones. That's why I don't bother much about the surface, I guess. The only really neat thing about the surface is the way you can hide so much under it." Dr. Creevey jumped a bit, just then, suddenly surprised. "Now here's something interesting," he said, leaning back in. "A very powerful bond of sympathy... for... *an aunt*? No! A grandmother!"

Horus' face scrunched up. "Well, I did note it pained him to talk about his family... letting them down. And he did speak well of knowing many generations of his ancestors. It bears out he might have been close to his grandmother. But honestly, Lias, the best you've managed so far is to tell me something I can corroborate. I'm not sure I can put these seemingly random facts you're extracting to meaningful use."

Lias shrugged. "Maybe with time, Horus. I've only just begun to look this over. Why not give me a few days? I'm sure I could tell you all sorts of interesting things."

Horus nodded, stood. "Alright. I appreciate you looking into it. Good day, Lias." He turned to go, but only made it a few steps...

"...There is the matter of *payment,*" the graphologist called. "The economy's busted, I know, but that won't last. I'm really here as a *State* consultant, you see. Any work outside the department... well, that's *commission* work..."

Horus turned back to him. "No matter. How much?"

"85 pence," Lias answered, with something like a dangerous smile. "You can write me up an IOU for it. That ought to be admissible, even in the present legal situation..."

Horus checked his pocket watch. Quarter after 11. Very good fortune, he felt. All-in-all, he didn't much like the idea of leaving *anything* behind with Dr. Creevey, if it was in his own handwriting...

"According to the Deputy Constable, the so-called 'present legal situation' expired fifteen minutes ago." He put away his watch and grinned at Lias. "How about cash?"

* * *

"So what did you think of that new graphologist?" Deborah asked. Returning from other business, she'd intercepted Horus just before he could return to the lobby. "Was he a total looney?"

He shook his head. "Much worse than that... he seemed completely sane."

She squinted. "Pray tell what's wrong with that?"

"I don't know precisely. There was just something about him. Something I didn't trust..."

Deborah shrugged. "Probably just the goatee."

Horus looked askance at her. "You know about that?"

"I think the receptionist mentioned something about it..." Deborah recalled hazily.

"Well anyway, I'm glad to be reminded of my access to formidable counter-intelligence. More than the goatee itself, perhaps, I didn't care for how much he already seemed to know about everybody."

"And how about your client?" Deborah asked, quick to dismiss his vague misgivings. "What could Dr. Creevey find out about him?"

"Apparently, that he loves his grandmother," Horus shrugged. "And is partial to the color green."

Deborah gave him another look. "I thought you said this guy *wasn't* a nut?"

"You would have to have been there. I think his findings may be accurate... if not especially helpful. But now, how about your own errand? How did that go?"

"The appointment's all set-up," she answered. "Vesta says you're free to call anytime it's convenient. Here's her home address." She handed him a sticky note.

"Thank you. I think I'll make this my next stop."

Deborah folded her arms. "Really, Horus: I know handling your appointments is part of my job, but I'm not sure why you have to go there at all. She knows you finished looking over the books. She learned that much just talking to *me*."

"Ah, but don't forget: She wanted to *pay* me for double-checking them."

"Well, we were *both* involved," she said slyly. "I wouldn't have minded so much, having the check written out to me."

"But I would have. I don't want you unnecessarily tied up in any legal scandal."

"I could have just waited to cash the check."

He shook his head. "Not *that* legal scandal."

She groaned. "Okay then... *which* legal scandal?"

"An account imbalance... reported by an anonymous tipster."

Deborah's rather exasperated look melted into a knowing grin. "Ah, I see now."

"Anyway, I'd best be off," Horus said, pocketing the address and readying to be on his way. "But you know, Deborah, my plan does require you to pay one more visit to Vesta yourself, before all this is through."

"Why's that, Boss?"

"Well, when the time comes for it, you'll have to make good and sure she hears about my arrest."

Chapter 12

The carriage ride took Horus beyond the urban terraces of Mt. Norvein, first along and then into The Chalice – a natural shelf in the mountain in the shape of a wide, shallow basin. He knew the area for one St. Argonsburg's best agricultural annexes, and it was immediately plain to see why. Though Horus had no history of admiring lush vistas (being of a make indisposed to vegetables and suited to arid climes), he had to admit he was impressed with the sheer, overgrown greenness of it all…

…It was no wonder, then, that as he was passing a relatively small, shadowy lot – whose hunched and wilty trees were slowly casting off their brown-grey leaves – he found it a tad unsettling. Such a bitter scene of decay stuck out in The Chalice like a ghastly thumb. He privately wondered what poor sap had the misfortune to live there…

Naturally, no sooner than he put the question to himself, and the cabby veered down a path straight into the heart of the whole creepy place. Horus leaned his head out the window to see if he could get a glimpse of the manor of the estate, but to no avail. Past the many rows and columns of the dead and dying little trees he could only make out something like a woody mesh fence, screening whatever desolation lay beyond.

Finally, the carriage passed under an arbor, and Horus could see the house. True to form, it was squat but wide, surrounded by an inner bastion of dead shrubbery, and loosely coated in thoroughly distressed, moldy siding. There, standing on the front stoop, all in her usual mourner's shade of black, was Vesta Djerkovic …

…Not that she was just idly waiting for him to show up, in point of fact… though that might've gone nicely along with the rest of the disconcerting turn the trip had taken. No, she was addressing another visitor… some kind of errand-runner, it looked like. They were in the midst of discussing something as Horus stepped out of the carriage. With his ears trained forward, he caught what amounted to the end of the debate…

"But you've already picked the place over. What does Mr. Concordio want now? The property itself, I suppose?"

"He does," the man answered. "He's willing to offer a fair price on it."

"Well then…" she said, smiling her impenetrable smile, "in that case, why don't you go back and tell him he may have it?"

The errand-runner looked rather shocked. “Really? He can have it… just like that?”

“Why of course he can, Dear.” Her tone was angelic, her teeth shining for all to see. “Over my dead body.”

The errand runner blanched. “Okay,” he managed at length. “I’ll let him know…”

Horus passed the wide-eyed man on the path as he went to take his turn confronting Vesta. This was, perhaps, a good reminder of how careful he was going to have to be… how easily the impending conversation could go horribly wrong. For by now, of course, Horus *knew*. And she would *know* he likely knew. But he couldn’t come right out and let her know *how much* he knew. Even with copies of the reports still intact, the banks had destroyed some of Horus’ hard evidence. There was enough, perhaps, to implicate Vesta. That wasn’t enough. He would need to show *how* she did it…

…And, if he played his cards right here, he’d come away with precisely the means…

“Good afternoon, Mrs. Djerkovic,” Horus called.

“Ah! Good afternoon, Mr. Templar,” she called back. “So nice to entertain more pleasant company for a change… you, and that extremely famous secretary of yours earlier.”

“I’m glad to know you think better of me than your other caller,” Horus said, looking back over his shoulder. “You handled that, shall we say, interestingly.”

She nodded. “My father taught me to always have a joke and a smile. Only I was never any good with jokes. Why don’t you come in and I’ll get you a glass of lemonade?”

Horus took another quick, curious scan of their withered surroundings. “Lemonade, you say? Not… *grape juice*?”

She shook her head. “I won’t have a *drop* of it on my property. Not ever again.”

* * *

“I learned something rather disturbing from your secretary this morning,” Vesta said, filling a glass in front of Horus with a sweaty pitcher of lemonade. “She told me the banks destroyed all their records during the economy outage.” She searched him with a look that was not so smiley. “Does that, by any chance, mean our little case is going to be thrown out?”

He shook his head. "No. When I informed Judge Felix that the second audit was complete, he went right ahead and set a date for court to reconvene. You'll be getting the notice in the mail before the day's out. It's Friday, at 8:00, if you care to know now." He eyed his glass a bit unsure.

She sat at the table across from him, gaze still fixed. "But what about *evidence*? How will you and the woman from the District Attorney's office argue out a verdict if all the records are gone?"

"Ah, but the State already retained all our records. And they didn't take the same total-war approach as the banks did. Your testimony can still be backed up by the statement and ledger. Otherwise, I'm sure Felix would've felt compelled to dismiss the case."

"That would have been *insufferable*," Vesta almost mumbled before taking a hearty draw on her own lemonade.

Horus politely followed suit. No sooner than the first drop hit his tongue, he felt his entire face shrivel up. "Hmm," he managed, after his mouth muscles relented their death-grip. "A bit on the sour side."

"That's what makes it real, Deary," she explained, finishing her glass.

Horus settled back into a more relaxed posture in his chair, both in segue and to put some distance between himself and the mere smell of the lemonade. "There are some layers of irony here, I suppose I can't help pointing out. Here I am, sipping lemonade in the home of the woman the State chose to audit a vineyard... coincidentally, a former vineyard proprietor *herself*."

She looked at him, betraying only subtle surprise. Horus kept an impassive front, though now he was truly playing the dangerous game. As before, he couldn't let her know he'd deduced her whole scheme. But at the same time, he needed to at least let on that he *might* be wise to her motives. Yes, perhaps what he needed to do was just a bit too nuanced. But then again, maybe that was part of what made misdirection so artful...

"No coincidence there, Sonny – that's *qualification*. My Richard ran this place until he passed – about forty-two years. But, the grapes are all gone now, as he is – practically *stolen*. The State didn't want good vines going to waste, so they were all transplanted to other vineyards."

Horus' brow furrowed. "You weren't simply expected to care for them yourself, after his passing?"

She laughed mirthlessly. "Goodness, no. I was the bookkeeper. And anyway, we lost the business." She gestured rather dismissively around them. "This was small peanuts next to a *grand* place like your *Vineyard 359*, you know. It took all the elbow grease and cleverness we had to keep it up as long as we did. And we almost pulled it off, too." Her gaze meandered sadly across the walls, trying to get at all the history in them. "But well, that's the past. The important thing to the State is that, after almost half a century's experience, I know business ledgers."

"I suppose you would," Horus said solemnly.

As they both sunk into a somber quiet, Horus inadvertently lost steerage of the conversation. Soon enough, Vesta made him pay for it with a perilous question...

"And, speaking of ledgers... won't you be a dear and tell me what you found? I'd still like to foot the bill for your audit, Mr. Templar, but don't keep me in suspense until Friday. I'd like to know now."

Horus got all bound-up inside. It was inevitable this would come up, but even so, it was hard to grapple with. This was the most tenuous point of their meeting. Any tiny misstep could blow everything...

"It was a curious thing," Horus began. "The ledgers seemed immaculate. I was as stumped as you were, trying to figure what they recorded wrong."

She raised a brow at him. "*Ledgers*?" she asked. "As in, plural?"

Dianodes, Horus privately cursed himself. He didn't even realize... he'd just tipped her off that he'd looked at books from more than just the case he was officially working. It was an awful mistake. For Horus, the primary danger of these cat-and-mouse conversations was usually just to resist the temptation to see how cleverly he could insinuate all that he knew without blowing the whole thing. But here, he'd just plain-old slipped-up. Now, he'd *really* have to play it cool...

"As a matter of fact, I have been looking at books from several cases," he admitted. "Vineyard 359 is not an isolated incident, it turns out. The State thought, since I was going to look at one set of books anyway, they might as well try their luck and see if I could identify a larger pattern." So far, his cover was true, which was always the best kind of cover.

However, Vesta still appeared deeply skeptical. "Well... did you?"

Yes, he most certainly did. Whether it was smarter to deny it or not, he could hardly decide on such short notice...

"I *may* have," he replied. "Honestly, I begin to think all these cases are just indicative of a problem at the bank itself. They seem to be reporting some deposits in a way my consultant didn't recognize... maybe erroneously."

Clever, Horus, but maybe not clever enough, he reflected. She'd likely accept his explanation. But, if she was *too* accepting of it – if she fully believed he'd committed to the banks as the problem, and didn't feel at all threatened any more herself – then she might just pay Horus off, and slip away scot-free...

For better or worse, she finally relented her search of his face, and went once again for her checkbook...

"That's an interesting theory, young man," she said, even as she began to pen one future or another. "I might have to give the statement another look myself. These old eyes really aren't *quite* what they used to be." She paused her writing. "How much?"

"One audit goes for 30 pence, I believe. But you would know better than I."

She shook her head. "But you just said you performed multiple audits..."

"Yes, but there's no reason to bill you for all the others." He raised one of his own brows. "Is there?"

Vesta blinked. "Nope!" she said, finishing the check. She tore it out. And then, slowly, from behind the iron curtain of her smile, she extended it to him...

Horus took it, folded it and put it in his pocket without so much as a peek at it. Not that it mattered so much anymore, but he'd already decided to act oblivious to her scheme and methods, and it was only good form to follow through. "Thank you, Mrs. Djerkovic. I'll take this right to the bank."

She nodded. "Please do, Deary. Please do."

* * *

It wasn't until he was safely riding away, and had passed the wall of trellises and an echelon or two of dead trees that Horus finally reached back into his pocket and pulled out the check. He'd awaited this with breathless anticipation... the moment that would, *hopefully*, confirm his theory, on which he'd staked the entire case. He carefully unfolded it. His eyes shot for the amount line. Then, his face drew up. Right there, waiting for him at the beginning of the line, was precisely the subtle little character he'd hoped to find...

"Well, that's that," he muttered to himself, returning the check to its former place. "Not much left of this case but to cross the finish line."

His sense of imminent victory was to be short-lived. After sparing himself hardly a moment of satisfaction, he found he was already staring blankly out the carriage window...

"But now, what about my *other* case?"

Chapter 13

The problem of Rythigaar was to steadily haunt Horus for the next couple of days. In all his years of studying and practicing law, he'd never before come up against or given serious thought to the plight of a man facing life behind bars. In the world at large, it was an unusual prospect, to be sure. But in *Jast-Madiir*, it simply wasn't done. People were either acquitted or otherwise disposed of in a speedy manner. In some cases – much to Horus' grave displeasure – convicts were even tried and sentenced in advance of their own arrest. Jast-Madiiran justice was a well-oiled machine, if not a flawlessly ethical one. So if nothing else, Horus was very used to deadlines – to time being of the essence. But for Rythigaar, the only tangible deadline Horus could point to was death by old age...

As that particular milestone was surely several decades out, Horus' real agony was over the invisible deadlines – the ones in the heart and mind. How long did he have before Rythigaar's hope failed him... before he resigned completely to an existence of slow decay in jail? Given he had been inclined to that notion from the very first, the answer was assuredly not very long. Worse yet, how long did Horus have before his own hope ran out? Before the situation normalized, and he became complacent, even *comfortable* with the knowledge that he had a client locked up in a little cell someplace? No... he most certainly couldn't let *that* happen. Even with seemingly all the time in the world, Horus was desperate to make something happen, and soon. No pressure at all made for an awful lot of pressure...

"But what to do?" he demanded of himself aloud a second time.

Deborah set her newspaper in her lap. "Pardon?"

"Oh, just muttering to myself again," Horus sighed.

She just smirked. "Sorry to eavesdrop on you and yourself."

He shook his head. "Not at all – I was hoping you'd jump in with us. We could use a second opinion."

"It's Rythigaar again, isn't it?"

"It is." He stood and walked over to the window of his car, where he could most effectively cast a contemplative gaze. "Not for the first time this week, I find myself caught between two alternatives, and neither of them offer any clear path forward. The Inquisition won't exonerate him. I'm up against nine centuries of tradition there... and rules that overshadow any law. But what about our own justice system? They've ignored every attempt

I've made to force the issue. In essence, each of his accusers wants to confer his fate on the other."

"That's one dandy catch-22 alright." She looked at him questioningly. "What was the other one?"

"Well, never mind about that," Horus quickly dismissed. "I haven't even got to the worst of Rythigaar's problems yet."

"Alright. What's the worst of it?"

"Even *if* I can somehow get him out of jail, he'll still be a prisoner of the past. He sees no future for himself. Nor can I seem to dream one up for him."

"That's going a bit beyond your job description, isn't it?" she tried to laugh it off. He didn't reply, only continuing to stare blankly out the window...

"...There *must* be something – something about his flight to the docks you could go on," she volunteered somberly, at length. "Didn't he have some destination in mind?"

Horus turned back toward her, grinning weakly. "Nothing more specific than 'away,' I'm afraid."

She stood, and came over to meet him in front of the window. "Alright. So he wanted to get *'away'*. Let's work with that. What's the farthest place he could go?"

Horus liked her spunk, alright. He doubted this would lead to any breakthrough, but it beat no lead at all. "The continent, I suppose," he replied. "Of course, that would mean flying into a whole new set of uncertainties. It's a long journey for anyone to make alone. And I doubt he'll find anyone else willing to go. The long silence from that part of the world has certainly grown rather ominous."

She shrugged. "Maybe that's just as well to him. Maybe he wouldn't mind sailing straight into potential disaster. Maybe he could find new purpose, trying to help with whatever it is that's been causing the disconnect."

"Maybe that's a lot of maybes," Horus goaded her. "The disconnect might not be on the continent itself, but in between here and there. We might send him straight to his doom. And even if he reaches that distant land, his former life will still be there waiting for him. There's no place in the civilized world untouched by the Inquisition. Certainly, none that we know of."

"Well, it was just a thought," Deborah sighed.

"And a more complete one than any of mine, at that," Horus assured her. "I can run the idea by him, the next time I see him – see what *he* thinks. If he likes it very much, none of my reservations will matter. Still, I can't help wishing for something more on-the-nose – some way he could salvage a piece of his former life and carry it forward meaningfully."

"Nothing the graphologist found was any help?" she asked.

He looked perplexed. "No. I already gave you the highlights from that meeting... basically a grab-bag of random facts."

She went for a stack of envelopes on one side of his desk. "Evidently you didn't check your mail yet today," she said. "There's a letter here from a Dr. Milt Creevey..."

Horus' eyes bugged. "What an oversight on my part. Let's have a look!"

She handed him the envelope, which he effortlessly clawed open across the seam. He unfolded the letter, reading as fast as his mind would permit.

"Well?" Deborah asked, after a while of watching his eyes slow and his face unbury itself from the letter.

"Hardly better than what he told me from the first," Horus lamented. "Rythigaar has a ragweed allergy and some trouble with reading comprehension. But mostly, the doctor just goes on about *the grandmother* again – how he's always cared so much about her, in spite of her treason."

"*Treason*?" Deborah demanded. "That's a big word to throw around. Strange, too... that he would have a relationship with a relative who's done wrong. We already know the Inquisition disowns the ones that don't follow the rules."

"The *treasure-hoarders*, at any rate," Horus corrected her. "But you're right... it *is* curious. But it seems like Art did mention something about the outpost being a former political prison of some sort..." He stopped as another thought struck him mercilessly. "Art! I haven't checked in with him in days... after he clearly had a dreadful night out with Ms. Cordon." He shook his head. "And I call myself his friend. Have you heard anything, Deborah? Is he doing alright?"

"Yeah, I'm okay," said Art's voice, much to Horus and Deborah's sudden surprise. Their eyes swept the office car, finally falling on another newspaper as it folded down, revealing the face of Art Mallard himself. He'd been in there all along, inconspicuous – using his finely-honed powers of anonymity to render them completely unaware of his presence.

"Well, speak of the devil," Deborah snipped, not greatly relishing such sudden surprise. "Next time you want to talk, Art, please run it by me first.

At *least*, don't go suddenly appearing out of the blue like that. I'm not supposed to let just *anybody* into Horus' office, you know."

"Nice to see you too, Sugar Snap," Art replied. "And anyway, it's not that I really wanted to *talk*, per se. More like, I was curious if *you guys* wanted to talk. Capeesh?"

Horus nodded. "I think I understand well enough. At any rate, I'm glad you're here, Art. I have been wanting to extend my condolences. I take it things didn't go well with Blucille the other night."

Art huffed. "I can't begin to tell you how bad. Nothing went right. And in the end, it turns out she had me figured for a big jerk all along. Even a fun date would've only ended in disaster..."

"I'm truly sorry, my friend," Horus assuaged him. "I know you really had your heart set on Blucille."

"Darn straight," Art said, folding his big arms, looking around evasively. "I can't seem to stop thinking how crummy it all turned out. I walk through the city and I see all the Humans... and I think, 'These people don't know how easy they've got it. They just get an order in the mail one day, hop in line at the marriage office, and come home with a spouse.' They don't even know what heartbreak is. Let me tell ya... it's a real sucker-punch."

"I'm sure," Horus nodded. "But you can bounce back. You'll meet another lady, when the time is right."

Art shook his head. "No... no I don't think so... and maybe that's the worst part of it."

Horus' brow furrowed. "What do you mean?"

Art hesitated, either collecting his thoughts, or wishing to dismiss them. "I mean, what happened that night was bigger than the bad date. It was more than Blucille's rejection. It's... it's hard to describe, but... I felt like it was a *message*. You should've been there, hearing that Primary Administrator Hihvnor go on about wanting *more* in life. How he made it sound like a sickness. And I have to admit, it struck a chord. For a long time, I've just had this sense that there should be *more*. At first, I just tried to fix it with impulse-buying. Didn't help. Then, it finally dawned on me... what I was *really* missing was a swell dame... maybe a few pups down the road. But it turns out I was wrong. The problem was never that I didn't have what I wanted. The problem was me wanting anything to begin with. So Blucille and I butting heads wasn't just some speed-bump on a longer road to wedded bliss. It was inevitable. It was a *reckoning*." He sighed, utterly dejected. "There's no future Mrs. for Art Mallard. That's his punishment for being selfish."

After hearing all this, Horus was beside himself, grappling with a peculiar mixture of sympathy and amusement. He'd never seen Art try to reason out matters of deeper meaning before, and it was obvious he lacked experience. But, to his even greater amusement, Deborah was the first to answer him...

"What a bunch of baloney," she said, resting her hands on her hips.

Art looked up from the floor, confused and a little disgusted. "What?"

"You heard me. I said *baloney*. Next thing, you'll tell us the words 'forever alone' popped up in your bowl of alphabet soup."

"We didn't even have soup," Art argued.

"You know what I mean," Deborah pressed him. "Come on, Art. You had a really bad night... no less at the tail end of a day that was a mess in itself. That doesn't mean the universe was sending you a message. You've always been very smart and perceptive, but you're no clairvoyant. Honestly, the only way to be absolutely *sure* you'll never meet the right woman is for you to give up. Think about it for just a second: Even if you're doomed to be lonely, what's the worst that can happen if you keep trying anyway?"

Art's eyes turned up to the ceiling as he considered the question. Then he shrugged. "More loneliness, I guess."

"Exactly," Deborah clinched her point.

"I concur," Horus finally put in. "I think you read into Hihvnor's rebuke of excess a bit too far."

"Maybe," Art said noncommittally. "I just don't know. It still gives me the willies, every time I think about it..."

"Perhaps you shouldn't entirely excuse it, then," Horus suggested. "Maybe there *is* some area of your life that could use a little moderation."

"Okay. Like what?"

Horus thought a moment. "Well, you keep talking about all the money you've been spending on nonessentials lately. How much do you think you've spent frivolously, just in the last month?"

Art ran the numbers in his head. "Probably not much above 14 G's."

Horus blanched. "See now, *there* – I think – you could do with a bit more restraint."

"If you say so," Art said, sounding unconvinced. "Anyway, I'm glad I talked to you guys after all. It's really been horrible, the last few days, feeling doomed. This is the first real relief I've had."

"Well, don't suffer in silence next time," Deborah told him. "We're here for you, you big dumb lug."

Art smiled. "Thanks."

"It's nice to see someone's prospects brighten," Horus chuckled. "As for myself, I can't seem to help always returning to Rythigaar. I still have no idea how to help him..."

"You don't have to tell me; I heard the whole thing," Art explained. "And you were right: I *did* tell you the Outpost doubles as a prison."

Horus squinted. "*Doubles*? Do you mean to say they still have prisoners there?"

"The creepy door lady said, 'A prison it was founded, and a prison it remains.' Those were her exact words."

A prison it remains. This seemed an extraordinary fact for Horus to have overlooked. It piqued his curiosity, to say the least...

"Who could they be holding there? And for what possible reason?"

Art shrugged. "The only inmates she mentioned were people they'd caught trying to join up with Galahadron Mucolyptus and his Dark Inquisition."

"That's what I thought you'd said," Horus nodded. "But all that was centuries ago! No one could have survived all this time..."

He paused, clutching his letter from Dr. Creevey, as it occurred:

"...No one, that is, except an Avarican."

Deborah lit up with sudden understanding. "The grandmother!"

Horus grinned down at the timely dispatch in his hand. "Talk about your signs from the universe. I would very much like to meet this mysterious ancestor of Rythigaar's. I feel distinctly that the experience would be most enlightening."

Art protested. "Now hold it, Horus. You just got done convincing me that signs are usually a bunch of hullabaloo. Don't go falling into that trap yourself! If this 'grandmother' is really a secret prisoner left over from the dark ages, do you think the Inquisitors are just going to let you waltz in and chat her up?"

KNOCK-KNOCK-KNOCK

Before Horus could answer, there was a knock at his door. Art searched the other faces in the room, wondering who it could be. But Deborah and Horus exchanged a look, feeling confident they already knew...

"Do you want me to get that, Boss?" Deborah asked.

Horus waved her on as he began to cross the room. "Let's both."

As he opened the door, it turned out to be none other than their friendly neighborhood police captain, Alexei. He stood on the car's veranda, looking disturbed.

"Mr... Mr. Templar, Sir," he began, nodding. He belatedly tipped his bobby at Deborah. "Ms. Boulevard."

"Hello Alexei," she replied. But he looked back wide-eyed at Horus.

"There's a spot of trouble, I fear, Sir."

"...And you're here with a warrant for my personal receipts and checkbook, is that right?" Horus continued for him.

Alexei went from looking much-troubled to downright shocked. "Well... as a matter of fact, yes. We have reason to believe that..."

"...That my own book-keeping will show a different balance than what the bank reports?"

"...On the word of an anonymous tipster?" Deborah added.

Alexei declined to offer any answer beside a few incomprehensible attempts at forming a question.

"Never mind, Captain, it's alright," Horus assured the man. "Just give us a few minutes, and we should be able to round up everything you're after."

In the time it took him to say that, Deborah retrieved a leather checkbook cover already bound to a stack of paper receipts. "Here we are," she said, sticking it in his hands.

"...But..." Alexei said.

"Now, Captain, I've cooperated fully with your investigation," Horus interjected. "And I trust that you'll find me cleared of any suspicion. Now, are you going to insist that I follow you back to the station, or can I be permitted my liberty while you prove out my innocence? I'm a busy man, you know."

"Ah... well..." Alexei said, simply unable to work out how Horus and his secretary had apparently – perhaps even joyfully – anticipated everything he had come here dreading to do. "I... I suppose I have everything I came for, here," he answered finally, examining the stuff in his hands. "We have no charge yet... only suspicion. So I'll permit your liberty, Mr. Templar. Only, don't leave the country."

"Very well... let's you and I make a deal," Horus suggested. "You promise to turn my finances over to anyone *other* than Vesta Djerkovic, and I'll promise to stay national."

"I... I can arrange that. Not that you're in any place to bargain, mind you, but..."

"...Goodnight, Alexei."

"...Goodnight," Alexei replied, weak and belatedly, only just before the door was closed on him.

Horus and Deborah turned back – sharing smirks – to an apparently empty room. Then Art put his newspaper back down...

"What was that all about?" he asked.

"Just another phase of the Vineyard 359 case," Horus explained.

"That went better than you let on," Deborah reflected. "Do you still want me to tell Vesta that you've been arrested?"

"Oh yes," Horus answered. "I meant for her to believe that regardless."

Art just shook his head. "You guys lost me."

"We did, for a moment," Horus said, eyeing the newspaper. "Why disguise yourself again? Are the police looking for you, too?"

"I just didn't feel much like talking to the man who doesn't appreciate good fingertip grooming," Art reasoned.

"I see. But now, back to the business at hand: how to arrange to speak with Rythigaar's grandmother..."

Art shook his head. "I'm telling you, drop it. It can't be done. There's no reason to even try."

"Ah, but there's every reason," Horus countered. "All of us – Rythigaar included – are bereft of inspiration for his future. We can't imagine where he should go, or what he should do. But I ask you: Who would have a clearer vision for a young man's life than his own adoring grandmother?"

"Literally anyone," Art asserted. "Ask Yuri the meat-market guy. Ask a barber. Get the Clerical Dronehood to conduct a survey. But forget this grandma thing. You couldn't meet with her if you were invisible."

Invisible, Horus meditated, even as his gaze settled once again on Art's newspaper. *Yes... yes, that's just what I'll be...*

Art evidently read the mischievous inspiration as it illuminated Horus' face. "Oh, no!" he protested, hurriedly rolling up his paper and putting it out of sight. "Don't even dream it, Horus! Not in a million, billion years!"

"Don't worry, Art," Horus comforted him. "It's not what you think. I won't ask you to go yourself. You've been through enough lately. But tell me this: the trick with the newspaper: can you teach *me* to do that?"

Art and Deborah both looked mortified at the question. Even so, Art was eventually obliged to answer. "In theory, I *could*. But it's no cakewalk, Horus. It took me *years* of intense training to master..."

"Perfect," Horus replied, checking his timepiece. "I give us till sundark tonight..."

Chapter 14

It was the kind of night that could chill a man to the bone. The wind whispered sweet oblivion through birch and poplar, while swaying branches cast an eerie veil between Horus and the stars. Somehow, the earth seemed old and bitter here, and reticent to grudge the living their business. And yet, he would have greatly preferred to stay in that overgrown bend of the road, rather than face the fortress beyond, blacker than the night. Never before had the sight or thought of it troubled him. But just then, at the edge of the wood, it nearly stole his icy breath away.

For a while he tarried there, in the last shadows of the trees. There were a few specially poignant moments of doubt, where his mind tried to pull him in many directions, and none more urgently than back the way he came. But he was disciplined, and focus prevailed. He took out and unrolled his newspaper, reflecting on all that Art had taught him over the past few hours. Of paramount import, the veteran private eye had revealed that the key to absolute anonymity – as it was to so many other things – was *intensity*. He said that if Horus could only stare *intensely* enough at the newspaper, he would be so incredibly inconspicuous that no one would have a prayer of noticing his comings or goings. Horus – feeling sure that, with just a little finesse, his own formidable courtroom stare-down technique could be modulated at the newspaper to achieve the desired invisibility – proved a confident pupil. They had progressed quickly from theory to application. Horus spent a couple of those hours pacing back and forth in front of Art, with his investigator pointing out subtle flaws, and generally refining his method with every pass. At the end of it, Art casually proffered on Horus the status of a very promising student who had already shown a good deal of improvement – after which he leapt into a rather undignified string of spirited appeals that Horus not go through with it...

But Horus would not be deterred. He would infiltrate the Inquisition outpost, search out Rythigaar's grandmother, and emerge enlightened. It was a plan too bold and simple to fail...

Recalling all this, the long and patient wait he had expected to make for just the right opportunity to spring for the front gate nearly came and went before his very eyes. Hardly had he hunkered by a specially dark and shadowy tree than the drawbridge of the outpost opened, and the gate along with it. The guard was being changed, this very moment! Horus would have liked more time for second thoughts, but he reasoned there would still be plenteous occasions for that on the march. He whipped open the newspaper with flurried action and, after boring into it with his most concentrated gaze, spurred himself to a speed-walk through the vast empty landscape between himself and the bridge...

The moments that followed were not the most comfortable of Horus' life. Between the sound of his feet shuffling over the gravel, the crinkling of paper in his shaky hands and the huff of his near-panting gasps for air, he felt about as inconspicuous as a one-man marching band. Worse yet, he had to sneak peeks at the ground below the paper just to be sure he was still on the path, for fear he would lose his bearing and wind-up walking straight into the moat. Art had strictly warned him that even the briefest aversion of his gaze could spoil the whole effect. Much later than he should have, he realized he could tip the paper up or down, so that he could at least get some idea what was in front of him using his peripherals. But by that time, it seemed impossible that his cover was not already compromised. Even so, he kept soldiering on with only the shadow of a *shadow* of a hope that the Inquisitors hadn't seen him. And even that exceedingly shadowy hope began to quickly diminish, as he heard heavy footsteps coming his way...

He took his first steps onto the drawbridge, holding his breath, the frigid night now suddenly stifling. The footsteps grew louder. They were closing in on him. He clutched the newspaper and stared at it with all his might. They drew even with him. He kept walking...

...And... finally... they passed him by. The guards kept right on their course to the outer watch stations. Suppressing gasps of relief, he passed another pair of guards... then another. He passed seven pairs before he reached the end of the drawbridge, where, at last, there was one final obstacle. He tilted the paper skyward and saw – almost too late – that the Door Keeper was directly in front of him! He narrowly missed the collision as he hop-stepped round the ancient sentinel, silent and stiff as a gargoyle. Fear, relief, and incredulity splashed each other in the adrenaline soup of his mind. Though he had quite nearly bowled the Door Keeper over, she took no apparent notice of him. And, in passing her, he had crossed the threshold... he had entered the fortress itself...

Horus darted for the nearest spot out of sight and caught his breath. He'd won an exhilarating victory. To have even made it this far was surely nothing short of a miracle. Even so, it was only the beginning. He flipped a page in the paper, where he'd stashed a detailed cross-section of the outpost Art had drawn for him. Referring to it now, though, the detail was slightly less than he'd cared to remember. Really, Art's diagram was no better than a doodle, bearing vague resemblance to a trash can wearing a big crown for a lid. There was an arrow pointing to the crown, and a label to go with it. "Fortress." There was also an arrow pointing to the can. It read "Queen's Prison." That was, perhaps, illustrative enough. It revealed that, of old, the Inquisitors had kept their prisoners in vast depths below the surface. Horus saw that he was going to have to delve deep. Moreover, if Art's diagram represented scale with any accuracy at all, he would have to delve *very* deep indeed...

But how to find the cellar? he wondered.

It was no simple query. The outpost was large, and he was no more likely to find a convenient directory than the stairway to the depths itself. And he couldn't very well ask directions. What did that leave him to go on?

Horus had only one recourse he could think of: He would have to trust his gut. For no conscious reason, he had a very distinct feeling that the natural place for a castle's deepest, darkest secrets would be somewhere in its westernmost annex. It fell well short of a hard fact, but after all, blind confidence had carried him this far. Training eyes, ears and snout furtively out of his shady little corner, he found the coast was clear, and crept stealthily round the bend, making for the west...

* * *

It wasn't long at all before ducking and darting alone scarcely sufficed to see Horus through the Outpost. Its halls were towering – its crossings like yawning cathedrals, with domed ceilings reaching to heights unsearchable in the dull torchlight. Many were the occasions when the newspaper was called upon again to see him across huge empty expanses. And the farther he wandered, the more miniscule he felt against it all – no better than a little mouse scurrying through one of the Czarina's mansions...

But even a mouse would have his ways of finding the cheese. While the search dragged ever on, with no markers of progress to point to, Horus' formidable constitution continued to fray. As immense as the space was, the acoustic environment of the fort felt terrifyingly crowded. The steps of wandering Inquisitors were carried to him on mischievous echoes, so that they hounded him from far off. A somber chiming sound like a distant piano recital haunted one gargantuan hall after another. Horus resolved then and there that if he ever made it out of this place, he'd do as little sneaking as possible for the remainder of his days. Sneaking – he decided – was too rough on the nerves. After enough of it – with his object no closer, and the path back to his starting point growing ever more hazy – it was much too easy to begin to feel that sneaking was all there ever was, and ever would be...

About the time he was truly desperate for some sort of break, the sound in the halls played an especially mean-spirited trick on him. A pair of Inquisitors rounded the bend right in front of him, and it was all he could do to throw the paper up in his face and hurl himself to the wall. As they passed him by, he listened-in while they conversed...

"Have you noted the convalescence in social structure lately, down in the Hollow?" asked one.

"Yes – as a matter of fact, I just came from there," the other answered. "They do seem markedly more organized than in past centuries."

When they'd safely gone, Horus folded back his cover. One of those Inquisitors had just come from "The Hollow." That was all he needed to hear to keep pressing on...

* * *

In the end, the way he sought ended up being distinctly more subtle than he might have hoped. When he'd reached what may have indeed been the very westernmost point of the outpost, he came up to a wall several stories high that sloped up and out until it reached a hard vertical edge. This rounded protrusion ran as far as he could see along the entire back wall of the fortress, and was covered over by a multitude of huge, riveted brackets... almost as if it were one big hinge that the fort itself could tilt on. Horus thought back to Art's trashcan-and-lid drawing, and his short account of how a Meduseldan Queen had once been held here, and it all began to make sense. And there... right where the bend in the north wall met the hinge... was a *door*... hardly larger than your average, Human-built door. This, he certainly hoped, was the path to The Hollow...

The door creaked slowly open in his grasp. He looked down. Directly on the other side of the threshold, he found the first in a series of steps leading down into darkness along a spiraling path. He could see nothing beyond the first dozen stairs. But he could *smell* an earthy mustiness – *hear* a sea of air slowly churning. He braved those first steps. He strained his vision, and braved a few more. And finally, rounding the spiral far enough to be looking directly back toward the underbelly of the Outpost, he could see vaguely into the depths of a truly, *extraordinarily* deep pit...

...But words like 'extraordinarily' and 'deep' hardly seemed to carry any weight here. He could *feel* the immensity of the hole in the ground, much more affectingly than he could ever hope to describe it. And, to be sure, much better than he could *see* it. Looking down, feeling utterly sick with vertigo, he couldn't even hope to make out the next step in the stairway. The only thing his eyes could discern in that utter blackness were a series of tiny, lazily floating little lights far, far below... dozens of little blue ones, trailing hypnotically behind single red ones. It was a slow and alien dance, and yet, timeless. Horus would have liked to just stand there and be mesmerized by it for a while. But he couldn't. He'd found the ancient prison of the Queen – and though it was huge and dark and featureless beyond his worst fears, he had his evidence that there was life down below. He was going to have to keep going. He was going to have to take another step, though he couldn't see it. And yes, there would be thousands more steps after. But as he squinted, squared his shoulders, puffed out his gut, and then... slowly... lifted his foot, he told himself all it would take was to muster the grit he needed in this exact moment... just to take that *first* step...

WHOOSH!

THWAM!

In a whirl of action, Horus found himself hoisted from his feet and pinned to the wall. He thrashed in a panic, but his fists fell on plated arms that wouldn't budge. He tried to call out, but even his breath failed him, his ribs under all the pressure of those ferally powerful and immovable hands. The best he managed was a grunt. But even as he struggled and sputtered, a voice sounded, bright and clear...

"Whoa, there, Mr. Templar!" the boisterous – and vaguely familiar – voice called at him. "A leap of faith is a very fine thing... but I fear what you were attempting was really more of a *plummet*."

Horus relented his thrashing, and the pressure abated enough that he could choke out a reply. "Hihvnor?" he rasped.

"Ha, ha!" Hihvnor laughed, about scalding Horus. "Yes, it is I, friend Templar." He let Horus down. "I am sorry that our meeting should be prefaced with such a vicious assault, but when I saw what you were about to do, I had little choice. Evidently, you couldn't quite see that you'd already reached the last stair in this little overlook of The Hollow. There was nothing beyond to meet your foot but empty space."

Horus adjusted his tie, regained his breath – rallying from manifold stressors. "Well in that case, I'm only too grateful you attacked me. But of all the astronomical chances! What are the odds you'd find me here, now, just in the nick of time?"

"They are quite good, I should think," Hihvnor replied. "The Door Keeper told me you had come to call. Oh, I did have a time of finding you, for a while. You didn't exactly wait by the front gate for me to meet you. But I eventually ran into some of my folk who told me they'd seen a Mesomela man, wandering this way and that."

Horus was floored. "The Door Keeper? She knew I was here? She *saw* me!? But... but then they... they *all* saw me..."

"Yes," Hihnvor admitted uncomfortably. "She did report that you were behaving most peculiarly. Silent, evasive... perhaps as if you were hoping in some way to avoid detection. But your utter preoccupation with that newspaper left her quite beside herself, even to venture a meaningful guess as to your disposition. I have been observing your comings and goings for a while myself, and I admit that I too am quite perplexed. Do you think you could explain the significance of the paper?"

"Well, never mind," Horus said, greatly embarrassed, pitching the dumb thing into the abyss. "Hopefully it will suffice to admit that, yes, I am indeed guilty of trying to sneak into your Outpost, Hihvnor."

"How very curious. Why would you do such a thing, Mr. Templar? Did I fail to convey at our last meeting that you are in very good standing with us, and most welcome here? Or, perhaps you feared we would hold against you the misfortune of becoming entangled in this business with Rythigaar, our estranged former brother?"

"No, nothing like that," Horus assured him. "Though it is on Rythigaar's behalf that I've come here." He paused, readying to attempt a last gambit... a moral confrontation. "I know about her, Hihvnor. I know about the grandmother."

As best Horus could make out in the near complete absence of light, Hihvnor nodded a slow nod. "Ah. I see. You've come seeking Imolkyr?"

"If that is her name," Horus replied. "I admit I don't know."

"And you evidently presumed that we would deny you visitation."

Horus blinked, only realizing for the very first time that that *had* been a presumption. "Yes."

"And so, it seems, you elected to secure that meeting by your own means instead."

"Yes."

Hihvnor sighed. "Well, I admit, I am rather disappointed, friend Templar. If not so much in you, then certainly on account of our own inability to project an image of honesty and transparency."

Horus knew immediate relief... though he also felt like a heel. "If I admit to being equally disappointed in myself, I hope that will make us even. Either way, I've come to meet this woman: Imolkyr. And now that you and I seem to have found one another, you can either arrange it, or else forcibly evict me. Otherwise, I can assure you I won't be persuaded to leave until I've probed the very depths of this fortress."

"I admire your conviction," Hihvnor replied. "But you are still holding on to one unfounded presumption. Imolkyr is not to be found down here. This was a holding place for the ancient Queen Huytut. It was not designed for our prisoners of average size. Rather, they were kept high above, in the towers. You have wandered in quite the wrong direction."

Horus sighed. "That figures."

Hihvnor slapped a big wiry hand on Horus' shoulder. "Come. I will show you the proper way."

"I would thank you to do that," Horus said. He didn't bother to let on how immensely grateful he was, just to be led back up those few dark stairs...

* * *

After leaving The Hollow behind – *forever,* he hoped, if not longer – Horus soon found himself in another deep space... this time, at the *base*, looking up. A pair of attendant Inquisitors were present to operate a hand-crank elevator that would take him to the pinnacle of the tower. They instructed him that the day's safe word was "blueberry," and that he was to speak it into a cup on a string by the wall when he wanted back down.

Hardly had he nodded his understanding, and the Inquisitors began to crank. He stood in that shaft for what seemed hours, listening to the immense chain curl over the sprockets just outside the wall...

When, at last, Horus reached the moody loft where the prisoner Imolkyr was kept, she was right there to catch his gaze, front and center. Under rays of pale light from above, she sat, as in meditation. It was a striking sight.

Horus had assumed that she would be dressed just the same as any ordinary Inquisitor. But her vestments weren't the familiar drab and dim shades of blue, brown and grey. They were stark white… so very pale that it seemed no color could touch her. Perhaps even more shocking was the mask. Far from the blank visage he was used to seeing, she had an elegantly sculpted visor, which, while not at all evocative of real facial features, seemed drawn down in a deep sorrow, rimmed all round with stygian settings like teardrops. She was, he understood, a sight from out of time… a relic from an age the world was blessed to forget. Hunched in her Avarican stillness, encircled by crimson tomes arranged like warding charms – each one a carefully-selected *Referendum*, no doubt – she could have been the very image of existential grief. To see her come unset and begin to stir was, admittedly, a little distressing…

"Who are you?" her ancient voice demanded.

"My name is Horus Templar," he explained. "I'm your grandson's defense attorney."

For a while, she only stared at him.

"…You, are aware of the trouble Rythigaar's in, are you not?"

"Yes."

They continued to examine each other in silence.

Horus cleared his throat. The burden was clearly on him to advance any sort of conversation. "I'm sorry if I disturbed you. Doubtless, a secret Inquisition inmate doesn't get many visitors."

"Few so exotic," she replied. Immediately after, a series of popping and cracking sounds emanated as her whole body began to quake. Horus was momentarily horrified that she might be falling apart. In fact, she was just standing up – a stiff struggle against countless scales that had apparently not been called on to move for a *while*. "I have not seen one of your kind since Ardillon the Rover pledged 5000 epsilons to our cause," she went on. "But you must excuse my poor courtesy. It is as you say – I have entertained none but my own captors for the last 45 centuries."

"That's…" Horus started, wanting to sympathize, though he was out of his depth. "That's a shame."

She turned up her palms. "It only follows logically. If I am a *secret* prisoner, as you claim, it is only because I have outlived any reason the world would have to remember me. One thing I have certainly learned in my days: Of the many great powers that shape our universe, Forgetfulness is not to be reckoned the least." She snapped and crackled, gesturing around at the empty room. "I apologize for the lack of furnishings. Would that I had a seat to offer you." Then, with effort, she stepped forward and stooped, retrieving one of the *Referendums*. "I could fashion you a makeshift out of these books, I suppose..."

Horus waved the idea off nervously. "That hardly seems necessary; I'm quite comfortable standing."

"But I insist," she said, already reaching for another book. "You may rest assured, Sir Horus Templar, that these will serve better at supporting your rump than they have in persuading me to renounce my beliefs."

* * *

Soon enough, they were both seated – Imolkyr back in her spot, and Horus propped up on a stack of tomes that comprised the Inquisition's canon. He found it far from comfortable, and not just because of the hardcover binding. Granted, in his lifetime he'd barely scratched the surface of Magormissahr's *Referendums on the World* (its dense volumes numbered in excess of a thousand), but like any civilized person, he regarded them as hardly less than sacred texts. It was another stark reminder of the remarkable nature of his host. The ancestral schism between the Inquisition and the Dark Inquisition was an obscure matter at best to him – one that presently inspired more curiosity by the moment...

"Now, you must explain what would bring a young legal professional here," Imolkyr began. "You understand I would know nothing of your country's law. It had yet to exist, when my stay in this place began."

He shook his head. "It's not a question of law that inspired this visit... though I admit, I could use help there, too. But I wanted to speak with someone who knew Rythigaar – someone who might be able to suggest a prospective future for him. All his life, he's known only the Inquisition. I'm afraid neither of us has had much inspiration, trying to imagine what he might do now."

She took a moment for consideration. "There again, I am unsure what help I can be. Temporal matters are not my expertise – my own future demands no consideration, and my past is only hazily recalled."

"But you *would* like to help him, if you could? The other Inquisitors... they prefer to behave as if he never existed."

She sighed. "Yes... that *is* the policy. Even for a Dark Inquisitor like myself, no other protocol was ever laid down. But Rythigaar – poor, impressionable lad – he was always so patient with my own apparent iniquity. He would hear me out – he would *speak* with me – when all others shut their ears. Yes, I would help him, were it in my power. And if that makes me a delinquent myself, it will be nothing new."

Horus grinned. "Well, I'm certainly glad to hear that. In fact, if all Rythigaar gains from this venture is the knowledge of your goodwill, I won't feel the effort was in vain. But now tell me: How did the two of you even come to associate in the first place? Surely not as part of a family reunion..."

"They send someone up here to give me food. They like to keep me well-fed, so that I may have more waking time to reflect upon the error of my ways. To them, it seemed an apt job for the boy – a Human, who would not likely live long enough to be corrupted by routine visits to a heretic."

Horus mentally registered a very empty serving tray beside her for the first time. "And, you eat this punishment-food? All of it?"

She nodded. "Certainly. Why should I refuse a morsel? Have I not betrayed my brethren's confidence, that I would remain steadfast in our doctrine? Even if it is because I have sought greater things, my punishment is deserved."

Horus was rather baffled by all this, and he knew he let it show. "My very limited knowledge of the Dark Inquisition isn't serving me well here. You've apparently rejected Magormissahran tradition... and yet in some ways you're still conducting yourself just as an Inquisitor would. If there's a distinction, I admit I don't see it."

"Did my casual treatment of Magormissahr's prose alarm you?" she asked, indicating the books beneath him. "It is not as if we have lost all regard for him. Rather, we see him for what he is... and is *not*. Magormissahr is wise, but not sovereign. His words were inspired by the Creators, not supplied by them. But Galahadron Mucolyptus bid us seize upon a chance to be reunited with the Creators *themselves*. In so doing, we might have learned deeper truths, or come to better understand our Purpose. But in any case, we would have bridged the gulf that was so ruinous – we would have basked once again in the radiance of Makers... and we would have shown them the deep scars of their long absence." She paused, and it seemed mournful. "I fear that Magormissahr revealed something of his true self by so hastily condemning these notions. But too few of us dared to recognize it..."

Horus found no small fascination in listening to her speak of these things. In all his schooling, he couldn't have spared the time to learn history as he'd learned the law, even if he'd wished to. But this was more than any history lesson. This was having a chat with a time out of memory: some of it forgotten by supernatural intervention, and the rest being too frightful to dwell on. "Tell me more," Horus said. "More about Galahadron and your crusade. I grant it isn't strictly on subject, but I think I can spare a while to listen. And after all, who am I to pass up an interview with a Dark Inquisitor? It's a rare chance, to say the least."

Her resigned posture became suddenly and almost imperceptibly more eager. "You may not understand what you are asking, Sir Horus Templar. If you could spare a decade to listen, I would endeavor to fill it."

Horus blanched. "Regrettably, my calendar is proscriptive. Do you think you could pare it down to an hour or two?"

She nodded. "Very well. But now, let me see what I can indeed recall..."

* * *

For not less than the next two hours, Horus immersed himself in her chaotic, extraordinary, and sometimes downright terrifying first-hand account of the Great Regression. That she had premised the tale by wondering 'what she could recall' turned out to be no idle segue. Such was the cataclysmic buildup of the time that total annihilation was only prevented by one of the elements of the universe coming forward to literally force people to forget all the ruinous Powers they had learned. The leader of Imolkyr's movement – Galahadron Mucolyptus – had evidently caused his rift in the Inquisition by proposing that these mysterious Powers be utilized to find and reach the Second Universe – the one the Creators had moved on to, after abandoning work on their original creation. Galahadron purposed to make war on this Second Universe, and – in that dramatic show of zeal – win back the attention of the Creators. Thus, he and his followers built Galahadron's Gate – a powerful portal through space, and all that lay beyond... between one Universe and another. Or, so they hoped...

"Wait a minute," Horus asked, his face all ascrunch. "You mean, you weren't *sure* the Gate actually reached to the Second Universe?"

Imolkyr made a popping shrug. "There was no way to know for sure, but to step through."

Horus reeled. "Talk about your leap of faith."

She nodded. "That was precisely the idea. Even if we could be certain that the Second Universe was attainable, we could not know in truth how the Creators would respond to our jealous assault on their new creation – whether they might look on us with pity, as we hoped – adrift and empty as we had been without them. There was all manner of questions both unanswered and unanswerable, when the Dark Inquisition made its great exodus. But all were secondary. What mattered was the willingness to *go*."

"Remarkable," Horus replied, quite genuinely amazed at the enormity of that one step so many had taken, so long ago. But then, a question of a more personal nature disturbed his muse. "What ever prevented you from going, if I may ask?"

She hung her head. "A moment of weakness, I suppose. It is a tale of some irony." She indicated the room again. "Do you know that I came here, to this dungeon, of my own volition?"

"Why?"

"I was part of a team which volunteered to remain behind for a covert operation – a gambit of long odds to free Queen Huytut of the Wuu Gappews, who was imprisoned here. If there *was* to be a war on the Second Universe, she would have been our mightiest proponent, save Opepci herself, who bore the very Tears of Creation across the Undervoid. It was a critical operation – a strategic military one – and lethal force was authorized. I was sure of my conviction to the cause... sure that, if need be, I could take the lives of my former brothers and sisters, should they stand between me and my object. After all, they were in error, and I had already pledged myself a warrior...

"But when the time came, I faltered. I could not do them harm. I failed to liberate Huytut, and was myself borne away as a prisoner." She was momentarily lost in somber reflection. "I suppose Rythigaar and I are very much alike, in that sense. We are both permanent captives to a moment of weakness."

A small smile crept up the flanks of Horus' snout, as the very inspiration he had come here seeking suddenly dawned on him. "You know, I do begin to see the family resemblance, now that you mention it. But since we have not yet answered the question of Rythigaar's future, why don't you tell me this, Imolkyr: What would *you* do, if you were suddenly loosed from this cage? What future would you seek for yourself?"

She regarded him. "That is no mystery at all, Sir Horus Templar. I would away to the Gate, at once."

"Naturally," Horus nodded, and said no more.

After a moment of empty soundscape spent pondering the relevance of his question, she sat more upright. "Ah. I believe I see what you are getting at."

"Yes, and how ironic it is. Just earlier today, my own secretary suggested Rythigaar sail for the continent. I dismissed the idea at the time – it seemed too far, and too hazardous... and presented no definite object. But now, I think I see the way for him to go. And it is infinitely farther, infinitely more perilous, and absolutely uncertain. But after all, I know his zeal for Purpose and the Creators runs deep. He'd never be content with anything frivolous. And I know he cares about *you*. I think he would be honored to complete the journey you could not."

She nodded solemnly. "I believe you are right, Sir Horus Templar. I believe that, should you propose he seek the Gate, he will not give a second thought. In all this, I am greatly pleased. I cannot convey my gratitude to you, for redeeming the life of my grandson."

He shook his head. "Don't thank me yet. There's still the unresolved problem of how to get him out of jail in the first place."

"I am confident you will find the way," she assured him. "Perhaps all it will take is steady pressure on the powers that be. His old Inquisition could extract him, if they would but lift a finger."

"Yes... but you know better than I what it takes to change their minds."

"I do... and it is a pity," she lamented. "If Magormissahran policy could only be examined objectively, I would first see them redress the matter of trespassers. For after all, we all have our moments of weakness."

"Sometimes I wonder," Horus admitted. "I think you erred earlier, when you characterized your own inability to do harm to another Inquisitor as weakness. And you've spent thousands of years up here since, upholding your cause."

"Yet you do not know how I have waivered, in that time," she cautioned him. "Oh, I put on a brave façade, inviting you to sit upon my *Referendums*. But in truth, I have had doubts, many times. Worse than that, I have entertained the idea of disavowing myself of the Dark Inquisition entirely, more than once... if only to see how it might alter my fortunes here. So I say again: We are all weak, at whiles. But to *bear with* each other's weaknesses – to encourage and strengthen, and work to reform one another – I like to think it would be a better way."

"As do I," Horus heartily agreed.

Imolkyr worked at standing again, which at least seemed passably easier than before. "I will detain you no longer, my good man. Your company has been a great boon – one that I hope will help to see me through centuries to come. But you have your responsibilities."

Horus checked his timepiece. "I do have to be in court tomorrow," he agreed. "And the night wears on. But you have my own thanks, Imolkyr. This is a meeting I won't soon forget." He faltered, grasping for a closing salutation that would be fitting. But, as he was about to leave her to a captivity with no foreseeable end, this proved difficult. "Goodbye," he said at length.

She nodded. "Goodbye."

* * *

Horus spoke "blueberry" into the cup and endured a trip back down the elevator shaft – one that proved much, *much* longer than the one he'd spent going up. For all the while, his conscience was beating him to a pulp. Eventually, he was forced to recognize the feeling he'd been left with, parting ways with Imolkyr...

I have another client, he inwardly confessed.

Even with that, the pressure didn't let up. He found himself rehearsing what he might say – how he might try to convince Hihvnor to let her go. He'd come up with little snatches that sounded persuasive, then bury them under new ones, all in vain effort to script the whole conversation ahead of time. But it was all a jumble, and he felt like a fool – no better than a man trying to prepare an argument with a stone...

But when the elevator finally returned him to its base, there was Hihvnor, still waiting for him. And somehow, all the reservation turned to resolution. He'd at least give it a try...

"That was rather a healthy chat you had, just now," Hihvnor said as he approached. "I hope you were able to find what you were looking for, my friend."

"I was," Horus replied, a bit stern. "But of course, when you leave no stone unturned, you invariably find more than you were looking for to begin with."

Hihvnor hesitated. "This begins to sound ominous. What more would you speak of finding?"

"I found Imolkyr *herself*, Hihvnor," he explained. "Granted, this is Inquisition business, and I'm only a lawman. I can do no better than argue with you about things I don't fully grasp. But that woman's been locked up there for over 4000 years. And I have to wonder: Where does it end? She might still be up there an eternity from now. And for what? Her movement has already passed on without her. She wishes for nothing but to go and join them, in whatever far-flung place they reached. What is she to you while she stays here, but a liability? A final hold-out of a rival doctrine that would have otherwise gone out of the universe long ago."

"You make good points, as ever, friend Templar," Hihvnor admitted. "And I begin to weary even myself by endlessly parading the same rebuttal: I have not the authority to do what you would ask."

Horus put a hand on Hihvnor's shoulder. "You have the authority of a Primary Administrator. Until Enscharaulgk's return, there's no higher authority than that to be found in this part of the world. And despite your inaction, I know you have a good heart to match. At any rate, the Grand Inquisitors entrusted you with the greatest power they could bestow. Perhaps it's about time you trusted yourself with it, too."

At that, Horus didn't wait for anything further from Hihvnor. He simply turned to go. No one called after or inhibited him. He left, revived and hopeful. Hopeful that, having discerned a course for Rythigaar, he would soon find the means for him to take it. And now, he had *more* to hope for, feeling confident that he'd placed his newest burden squarely on the shoulders of Hihvnor...

Chapter 15

The next day found Horus back undercover – this time, fortunately, behind the veil of a big wooden door, rather than a flimsy newspaper. He'd arranged to conceal himself long enough to let court convene, so that he could spring his ambush most effectively... or, at least, most dramatically. While he listened, with a tall ear pressed up against the cold mahogany, Judge Felix began, as agreed...

"Court is now in session," he called, clacking his gavel. "Let the prosecution witness be recalled."

"I call Vesta Djerkovic to the stand," Blucille Cordon announced as she rose. Horus didn't get to see the stoic but strangely present look on her face, nor the devious, self-satisfied new smile on Vesta's. But he could read the panic in his own client well enough, when next someone spoke out...

"Objection!" Boris the vineyard owner squeaked. "I mean... that is... we can't start this thing now! This is madness! There's no one here to defend me!"

"Hm, that *is* irregular," Judge Felix played along. He hadn't been a very good sport about this idea – as he tended not to be – but agreed with token urging. Horus wanted Vesta on the stand before she knew she'd been had – not *just* to catch her off-guard, but also just in case she was a flight risk. Not that she would likely get far anyway, but what she didn't need was a charge of resisting arrest to go along with everything else she'd done. No – far better that she just be made to answer for the crimes already at hand...

"We seem to be at an impasse here," Felix went on. "The defense council was to present the findings of his audit now, and cross-examine this witness by them..."

"It seems that young Mr. Templar learned a bit too much about this case for his own good," Vesta smirked, taking the stand regardless. "Got into a bit of financial trouble himself, or so I hear. Poor dear. He must've discovered how Boris here was confusing his records, and thought he could improve on the scheme. But, in the end, he got what all crooks have coming to them..."

"Did I?" Horus boomed, throwing open the courtroom door with a thrilling flourish. "And what, I wonder, would Vesta Djerkovic suppose she has coming for *her*?"

At last, the moment had come where Horus utterly destroyed Vesta's adamant smile, leaving her with the look of a hypsilophodont in the headlight of a speeding train. She quickly rallied, trying to paste her cheerful visage back together, but it was at best a jittery shadow of its former self...

"Why... Mr. Templar," she stammered. "I'm... quite surprised to see you. But whatever do you mean, 'what's coming for *me'*? My involvement in this case is strictly objective. I'm only the State's auditor..."

"*Voluntary* auditor," he corrected her. "One that I submit knows a great deal more about the financial imbalances in question than she's been willing to admit thus far."

"That's a big story," she challenged. "Perhaps your own audit turned up something my old eyes missed, Deary. If that's the case, good on you. But that's no grounds to cast suspicion on me!"

"As a matter of fact, my audit *was* somewhat more successful than I let on, when last we spoke," Horus revealed. "My secretary and I uncovered a good deal about the irregularities in the books of Vineyard 359. Theirs, and the books of the other nine cases you've also been handling for the State. Among other things, we found that you *are* more than just an objective auditor. In all ten cases, you were also a *customer*."

"You're lying!" she demanded. She turned to Judge Felix. "Are you just going to let him badger a poor elderly lady this way, Judge? Why, if my Richard was here, I'd have him..."

"...Yes... *your Richard*," Horus interjected. "The quintessence of this entire case. Of course, if only he *was* here, none of us would be."

She glowered at him. "What are you talking about?"

"I'm talking about motive. Yours – to defraud Vineyard 359, and most of the other major vineyards in the region. You blame them for the loss of your business and, ultimately, of your beloved husband. You yourself admitted to me that it was a *vineyard* the two of you used to run together – a small one, always scraping just to keep afloat in a big vineyard's game."

"That's a matter of public record," she huffed, folding her arms. "I don't deny it."

Horus reached into his jacket. "Here's another public record I hope you won't deny," he said as he unfolded a sheet of paper and set it on the stand in front of her. "Would you please tell the court what I've just presented to you?"

Vesta looked the sheet over with wide eyes. "It's... it's an application for a patent."

"In whose name?" he plied her.

She hesitated. "Richard Atterboron."

"Richard Atterboron," he repeated back to her. "Alias R. Atterboron, alias Rick, alias 'my Richard'. Either your own name or one or more of these appears on all ten books the state had you audit. Yet you claim I lied when I accused you of being their customer. Do you withdraw that statement, or do you wish to be liable for perjury?"

"Alright, so maybe I bought some groceries. And there's a lot of 'Ricks' out there, you know. I don't see how that proves anything."

"We can redress that later. For now, let's return to motive. You've read the name on the application. Would you please also tell the court the substance of it? What was your husband pursuing a patent for?"

She reviewed the paper... as if there was any chance she didn't know. Her voice grew soft, sensitive. "He... he wanted a patent on a new type of drink... infused with... little carbon bubbles."

"But the patent office rejected his application. And, of course, that was only the beginning of your problems. The carbonated grape juice sold well, for a time. You finally had your corner of the market staked out. But without patent protection, the other vineyards soon copied the process. They edged you out, without so much as a thank-you for the idea." His own voice softened. "In the end, you lost your business. And your husband was executed for mismanagement."

She looked up slowly, holding back tears. "Well... that *is* motive, isn't it?" she asked, trying to fix a weak grin. "Only you're forgetting one thing, Mr. Templar. The ten businesses. Not all of them are vineyards. How do you account for that?"

"Easily enough," he replied. "A simple smokescreen to conceal your true targets. If all the businesses reported by the anonymous tipster had been vineyards, that would have raised other questions, wouldn't it? You needed some oddballs thrown in to confuse matters."

"I suppose next you'll claim that I'm the anonymous tipster, too," she chided him.

"I believe you are," Horus admitted, nodding. "But whether you are or you aren't is irrelevant. It can't be proved."

"I'd like to see you prove any of it. You have your motive alright, and a plausible story. But *how* did I do it? It'll be a real dandy if you can come up with that one."

"It was with the checks you wrote," Horus explained. "You ingeniously devised a way to write a check that would act the opposite way of an ordinary check."

Vesta forced herself to laugh. "That's patently ridiculous! Checks only work one way, Deary. Less money for payer, more for the payee. How could it possibly be otherwise?"

"By turning a negative to a positive, if I may paraphrase something you once told me," he answered. "Or, perhaps more precisely, turning a positive to a negative. I grappled with the question myself for some time. During our audit, Deborah discovered there were negative deposits on the bank statement. Neither she nor I had ever heard of such a thing, much less encountered it. But on close examination we couldn't deny that some of the deposits had been written up that way... *in red*. We couldn't come to any working conclusion, except that you must've made the checks out in some unusual way."

She grinned again, venomously. "Is that all you have? A *conclusion*? That won't do, Mr. Templar. It simply won't do. Suppose you're right. Suppose I wrote some crazy checks. You'll remember, the banks destroyed all their short-term records. Those checks you allege are just ribbons now. You still have no proof!"

"But you gave me the proof yourself," Horus rallied. "Or, don't you remember? You worried I was on to you. So you thought you'd pull off one more frame-up. In fact, you prepared a contingency from the very moment I proposed a second audit. You reasoned that if I was mired in my own financial trouble, I couldn't very well point the finger at you. It was a bold gambit, I grant, but you ultimately sealed your fate with it. With *this*..." he said, taking out a small paper order. "A *negative* check!"

The crowd gasped... even though, from their vantage, they couldn't possibly see the check Horus confronted Vesta with... the very one she'd written him as payment for double-checking her work. They couldn't make out the tiny dash marks she'd written in ahead of the amounts, both in print and numerals, denoting a negative value. Nevertheless, the proof was there, just in front of her. She could deny them no longer, though she tried...

"But... but you didn't even look at the check. You said you'd take it straight to the bank..."

"And so I did. But by the time you had it written out, I already had your scheme figured. I'm not here on bail, Vesta. I didn't have the check deposited. I merely asked the clerks for their assessment of it. They told me definitely, as the amount written was negative, it would have to be assessed as money in *your* account, and out of *mine*. They would simply write it up as a positive withdrawal and a negative deposit, respectively. And that, my dear Mrs. Djerkovic, was the final end of this case."

He just watched her turn somber again, deflating as the totality of her failure sunk in. He hated to wound her, even with all she'd done, and all she *would* have done to him, just to get away with it. "It really was an ingenious malfeasance. The dashes were so subtle. Anyone receiving the check would only see the amount they were expecting. But the bankers – they wouldn't know what amount to expect. They would have to read more closely. And just as you hoped, they noticed your negatives. You nearly pulled off the heist of the decade... even if it wasn't for very much money."

"Nothing at all next to what they owed my Richard," she replied absently. "Oh, not that I didn't relish extorting even a little pocket-change from those villains. But the main thing was to see how much *trouble* I could get them into." She sighed. "Too bad it wasn't to be." Then she gave him a defiant look. "Well, this is indeed the ending you worked out, Horus Templar. The snooty businessmen go free, and you've caught a feeble old lady in her evil scheme. I hope you're proud of yourself."

"In a way, not really," he admitted. "I see there are injustices here that can't be resolved. But after all, Vesta, things could have gone worse for you. You *did* have serious malicious intent. *Some* punishment, at least, was probably in order. But that's not always how it goes."

Her brow knit as she considered him. "What do you mean to say now?"

Horus looked up at Judge Felix. "Well, it's not really for me to explain. Would you care to take it from here, Judge?"

Felix nodded, and turned to Vesta. "Vesta Djerkovic, you are ordered to remit the sums of moneys owed to Vineyard 359, as well as the other businesses, forthwith. Additionally, you are ordered to remunerate the moneys you gained from them in dubious fashion. However, since there is presently no law prohibiting the circulation of negative checks, no additional corrective action can thus be prescribed at present. Rather, the justice department is willing to wave any possible future charges of fraud brought against you, pertinent to revised legislation, as well as the serious offenses of false and perjured testimony – under one provision. Your services as an advisor to the State financial department are to be retained, forthwith. You will be taken immediately to the Royal Board of Financiers, there to give a full account of your fraud, and all that went into its execution. Furthermore, any future schemes to extort or otherwise secure moneys in a devious or disproportionately effective fashion will also, immediately, be fully divulged to the Board." He leaned over the bench. "Do you accept the terms of your acquittal?"

"Darned straight I do!" Vesta answered.

"Very well." Felix struck the table. "Sentence is carried. Bailiff, please see this woman to the Board of Financiers."

"Are you kidding me!?!" Boris demanded. "She almost got me in a world of trouble for no reason, and you're just going to let her off? *Hire* her, even?!"

"Oh, cut out the water-works, Boris," Vesta snapped back. "He *just* said, what I did isn't legally defined as fraud yet. You're lucky they're even making me give you the money back."

"Well, what about defamation?" Boris whined insistently. "She brought me in here on a false pretense! Her 'anonymous tip' was bogus!"

"But they never proved I was the tipster," Vesta argued, even as she and the bailiff reached the courtroom door. She shot him one last sickening smile. "It could've been anybody."

Horus was suddenly struck dumb. Vesta's words bounced around in his head… just as words often did, when they heralded epiphany…

"It could have been anybody," he repeated back to himself. "Yes. That's it. How did I not see it before? *Anyone* can press charges in this country. Anyone at all…"

"You muttering something to yourself again, Boss?" Deborah asked, taking note of him. He didn't reply, presently bolting for the bench…

"Your Honor," he appealed to Judge Felix. "May I request a one-hour recess?"

Felix gave him a look. "A *recess*? But… I just passed judgment. The trial is over…"

"That's all well and good," Horus nodded. "But really, your Honor: my recess: may I have it?"

Felix gave an incredulous shrug. "If it means that much to you…"

"Thank you," Horus said, then charged for the door. He called down the hall in a loud voice. "And thank *you*, Vesta Djerkovic!"

"No, Deary," she called back, too pleased with herself and her good fortune to wonder what Horus was on about. "Once again, my thanks to *you*!"

Before he could do anything more, Deborah stopped him in the doorway. "You're acting crazy, Horus. What's up?"

"No time to explain," he explained. "I have one hour to go and fetch my client."

She nodded back into the room. "Your client's back in there, still pitching a fit."

"Not Boris," Horus shook his head. "I need to go get Rythigaar."

Deborah beamed at him. "You figured a way to get him into court?"

"In the end, it was simplicity itself." He waved her on as he started down the hall. "Come with me, Deborah. In an hour's time, we'll be celebrating two victories for the price of one."

Chapter 16

If Judge Felix had been dubious of Horus before, when he'd suddenly called for a recess at the very end of a trial, his doubts were not to be quickly assuaged. Presently, he sat behind his bench, about to reconvene court, at Horus' urging. No one beside the court recorder was there to pay observance, save for Horus himself, his secretary, and some mysterious little man dressed as an Inquisitor. Felix eyed them each in turn with escalating incomprehension. The world-famous Deborah Boulevard looked back up at him, all aglow with a joyful countenance. Horus Templar's face was exceedingly cheerful and eager. The man – whoever he was – wore the neutral mask of his Order, and so was unreadable. By his posture, he did seem attentive, at least... though whether he was also anticipating something, as Horus seemed to be, or whether he was every bit as befuddled as Felix himself, there was no way to be sure...

"Court is back in session," Felix announced to the three of them, at last. "The defense is invited to explain his business. What more is to be added to the case of The State vs. Vineyard 359?"

"Nothing, your Honor," Horus explained, a rather evasive look replacing all that enthusiasm as he joined his hands before him. "Regrettably, I failed to explain that I had hoped to bring *another* case before the honorable Judge Felix, before I departed. Of course, I had only an hour to go and bring my client here from his detention. Given greater latitude, I could perhaps have been more forthcoming about my intentions. I hope your Honor will make a gracious allowance, in light of this time constraint."

"Well, never mind," Felix replied, already growing weary of Horus' inscrutable niceties. "What is this new case you present to me?"

"My client Rythigaar stands charged of petty theft," Horus announced. This seemed to come as some surprise to the Inquisitor, who alternated looks between Horus and Felix.

For his part, Felix took another look around the empty room. "Who out there brings this charge against your client, I wonder?" he asked.

"I do," Horus answered.

"You?" Felix blanched. "You are bringing a charge... against your own client?"

"Yes, your Honor."

"That begs... another question," the Judge reasoned, hesitating even to ask it. "Who will be representing you in this suit, Mr. Templar?"

"According to civic law, and by virtue of my credentials, I have elected to represent myself."

Now, Felix's mind was really set spinning. "So... let me clarify this point, Councilor. You propose to play the part of the defense council... the plaintiff... *and* the prosecutor?"

"Yes, your Honor."

Of course, the Judge was beside himself... an ironic turn of phrase, perhaps, considering Horus' present aspirations. But, rather than make a fuss when he truly had no idea what was going on, Felix decided to simply sit back and let the Public Defender put on his peculiar one-man show. "Oh, very well," he said. "Let us... that is, let *me* hear this case. What does the prosecution allege to be stolen from the plaintiff?"

"My nose," Horus answered, absolutely straight-faced. The Inquisitor was now trained on him steadily. It finally became clear that he had no idea what was going on either. Felix could only sympathize...

"Your nose?" he demanded.

"That *is* the allegation of the plaintiff, your Honor."

"Alright. Does the prosecution have an opening statement?"

"No, your Honor. Prosecution waves its statement."

"And... the defense?"

"Defense also waves its statement, your Honor."

"Good," Felix nodded. "I'd sooner keep this moving right along, if it's just the same to all of you. The prosecution may call its first witness."

At this point, Horus looked out at all the empty seats himself. Then he turned back to Felix, a crestfallen man. "Regrettably, your Honor, the prosecution has no witnesses to call."

Felix searched him. "What evidence, then, does the prosecution intend to present?"

"None whatever. It is, therefore – and with great reluctance – that the prosecution officially rests its case."

"I see." Felix would have turned to the defendant's table at this time, but he was already looking there. "What of the defense? What does it present?"

"The defense objects strenuously to the baseless allegations brought against my client," Horus went on. "It is my contention that the defendant's innocence in this matter is as plain as the nose on my face... if your Honor will pardon the expression. At any rate, the complete lack of evidence from the prosecution should be grounds enough to dismiss the trial. The defense therefore moves for acquittal."

Felix folded his arms. "Is that what you want, Horus? Do you want me to acquit this man? Will that positively end this charade?"

Horus nodded. "Yes, your Honor."

Felix smacked the bench a good one with his gavel. "The defense's motion is carried. All charges against the defendant Rythigaar are summarily dismissed. Court is adjourned."

Horus grinned, privately exultant. This victory had been won without fame, fanfare, shock or awe, and certainly less in the way of showmanship than he preferred, perhaps... but it was no less special to him. Yes, in the end, the solution had been painless. But he'd journeyed high and deep, and risked much, to make it to this simple resolution. And he'd redeem a client from what seemed so much worse than a swift judgment. He permitted himself just a moment of personal satisfaction. Then he turned to his client...

"Well there you have it, Rythigaar," he said, the man standing to acknowledge him. "No jail will hold you now. You're at liberty to go, wheresoever you will."

"I cannot thank you enough, Mr. Templar," Rythigaar said, nodding. "Your methods are indeed extraordinary. I *am* eternally grateful. And yet..." he hesitated. "...And yet I remain unprepared for this unlikely turn of fate. Where I go from here remains a question unanswered... and, I fear, unanswerable."

Horus clapped him on the shoulder. "Not to worry. The answer may be more forthcoming than you think..."

Chapter 17

The day of departure was not as bright and cheerful as Horus would've liked. Overnight, a dense grey fog had rolled unbidden up and off the Farjean Sea. Even now – near midday – they were in the thick of it...

As if things could have cleared up noticeably in the last few minutes, Horus drew up the blinds of his carriage window. Still almost nothing to see. His usual route was lost in an alien desolation, with shadowy figures wandering in and out of nothingness, and trusty landmarks reduced to hazy suggestions of their former selves. But the more he looked at it, the more he decided it was fitting. If, for only a moment, he could feel like he was venturing into the unknown himself, then that was nothing next to the journey they were about to kick off...

It would commence from within the Civil Headquarters building. Horus' comment about no jail holding Rythigaar any longer had been somewhat premature, it turned out. Acquittal came with a paper trail, after all... and the circumstances of this *particular* acquittal had made for a bit of a bumpy road. Horus' suit for his own nose had to be formalized after the fact, as did the trial itself, which he'd tacked onto the end of another trial rather informally. Felix's were not the only eyebrows to be raised in the process of securing Rythigaar's release. But, at last, the ruling of the judge was recorded to the satisfaction of all the bean-counters and pencil-pushers. Today they would pick him up, and send him on his way...

When they'd reached the department building and snuck out of the cab, Horus and Deborah crossed a shadow they recognized. It was the form of Art Mallard, leaned up against a streetlamp, blowing bubbles.

"Well, look who it is," Deborah called to him. "You decided to come after all."

"You kidding?" he replied, standing straight and casually shaking the rest of the soap out of his pipe. "Wouldn't miss it. This is a heavier parting for me than anyone."

"Yes, well, thank you for your brave sacrifice, Art," Horus said. "It *is* good to see you. Will you be coming in with us?"

"Is there a reason I shouldn't?"

Horus joined his fingers uncomfortably. "Well, I *will* be stopping in at Blackforest's office..."

Art shrugged. "No skin off my nose. I'm sure she-who-we're-not-mentioning will be too busy to notice my coming and going anyway."

"That's the spirit," Deborah smiled.

As they all started up the short stair to the front entrance, they were immediately stopped again, noticing the Deputy Constable in their path – unfettered, and on his way out...

"Good morning, Milo," Horus acknowledged him. "You're looking well. I trust you've been given the clean bill of health."

"Wrong as usual, Templar," Miloje replied, tipping his hat at Horus and Deborah. "Turns out my old ticker really is out of whack, after all."

Horus looked on with sympathy. "Alexei did explain what you were being tested for. I'm... sorry."

Miloje turned his hands up. "No need for tears. I'm not dead yet. Brighter still, I'm not tied on the end of a string to that Plague Doctor any longer. That's enough to make any man feel light as a feather."

Horus grinned. "In that case, I'm glad for you."

"And I for you, Councilor. I've remained apprised of your progress; you've outdone yourself of late. You bamboozled an old woman and got a guilty client acquitted. Surely, the stuff of dreams for a man of your profession."

"Now, be fair, Milo. My client *was* innocent of the only crime anyone would charge him with."

"Spoken like a true attorney," Miloje riposted, tapping the side of his nose. Then, he started on his way down the steps again, waving back over his shoulder. "Good day to you all."

* * *

Too soon, they were up there, crossing the District Attorney's office. Art tried to look around with cool indifference. But the casual trajectory of his eyes betrayed him, and his heart skipped a beat when he chanced to see her in her office, deeply entrenched as ever behind piles of case-work. He should have been too hurt to care. But all he really felt was pity. Pity for them both...

But when that unfortunate fraction of a second finally ended, he passed by a desk and into Blackforest's personal office with hardly a hitch in his getup. The DA rose from his own stacks of papers, smiling sharp teeth at them with his signature blend of confidence and menace. Blackforest, too, it seemed, was back to his old self...

"Hello, Horus, Art, Ms. Boulevard," he nodded at them. "Have a seat, if you like."

"Thank you anyway, Hamilton, but I'd sooner be in and out," Horus replied. "I've already lost my client precious daylight to sail by, waiting for this fog to clear up."

"Yes, it's too bad about that." Blackforest whipped a paper from his desk and waved it in front of them. "I've notarized his writ of release. They'll be watching for you, down in the detention area."

"Thank you, Hamilton."

Blackforest shook his head. "It's me who should be thanking you, Horus. You've cleared a black mark from this department. I don't think we needed a permanently-incarcerated Inquisitor on our books, any more than we needed an executed one."

Horus met his headshake in like manner. "I'll admit to being a little disappointed in you this time around, my friend. I don't believe you ever *did* give this case a moment of thought beyond the superficial scandal. You never looked below the surface."

You know, you're absolutely right," Blackforest agreed, eyes glinting with self-satisfaction. "And now, I'll never have to."

Art filed in behind Horus and Deborah, queuing to leave Blackforest's office, no sooner than they'd reached it. He shambled glumly out, eyes cast on the floor. They were already on to the next order of business. But he would have to go on remembering this pointless pitstop – the hollow feeling of walking past *that door*...

Presently, he heard a loud 'thump' on the desk he was passing by – a deliberately violent drop of a healthy stack of papers. Something unaccountable made him realize that the noise was meant to get his attention. He turned, and there was *Blucille*, staring him down from beneath her big hat...

The mutual gazing was brief but intense. Internally, Art was trying to rattle his words out of the dark corners they'd darted to, and see if maybe he could even string some together. Just about the time he opened his mouth, hoping something would come out, she held up her hand to stop him. Then, she reached into her handbag. And she set something small on the desk. He watched as she withdrew her hand. And then he saw it – the stalk of lavender he'd given her...

After considering it, he looked back at her, and their eyes locked again. "I've been meaning to let you know that I *hate* lavender," she said. "I find the smell of it practically nauseating."

Art was beside himself. He had no idea why she should be telling him this, nor could he reconcile it with the facts. His heart sank all over again: Maybe she was just picking another fight. But before he could ask, she went on...

"I only use lavender soap in my pipe because I know I let the habit get out of control. I figured, maybe if I used the most disgusting soap possible, it would help me dial it back."

Art pondered her words for a spell. Then, with sudden understanding, he grinned. "Guess I didn't know you as well as I thought."

"More to the point, you didn't know me as well as *I* thought." She folded her arms. "Here's something else you ought to know: I was a huge jerk the other night."

He nodded. "That I *did* know."

"Yes, but you earned the confession." She looked away a bit sheepishly. "I'd even like to make it up to you, sometime. That is, if the idea of taking me out again still strikes you. I'll certainly understand if it doesn't."

"Well, I dunno, Blucille. That is, I'm not really sure either of us is up to an encore. It *was* a pretty awful date."

She grinned back at him. "It was the worst date of all time. So, if you think about it, any follow-up would have to be an improvement."

Art could hardly help fully committing to a dopey smile, listening to her inspired reasoning. "Well, in that case, you're on, Dimples!" he said.

"Ooh-kay," she chuckled, still rather bashful. "What time?"

"Definitely sometime," Art answered. "Where should we go? Your choice."

She shrugged. "Someplace."

Art nodded, giving a thumbs-up and a wink. "It's a date!"

For as much as Deborah and Horus took note of Art falling behind, they didn't wait around to find out what happened, content for the moment to pass it off as none of their business, and having no reason to suspect anything but the worst anyway. Rather, they continued on to the detention area, where they found Captain Alexei waiting for them. Likely, they had been expected earlier. When they got there, the Captain was occupying himself with his nose in the newspaper...

"Ah, hello Ms. Boulevard and Mr. Templar!" he said, as he caught sight of their movement over his specs. "You've come at last! Have you had time to take in the day's stories? Some interesting scuttlebutt is afoot! Do you know the Czarina has just christened a new flagship? The *Ebenezer*, she dubbed it... no doubt for the late Czar, her grandfather. It is a curious ship, purportedly made of ivory."

"I know something about that," the voice of Art replied from behind them.

Horus whirled. "Ah, Art, you've caught up with us already."

"What on earth happened back there?" Deborah demanded. "You actually look peppy."

"It was *Blucille*," Art explained. "We're back on for another date! Turns out she hated lavender all along!"

Horus made a face. "You'll have to explain in greater detail later. But congratulations! The way you'd talked, I didn't suppose there was any hope left."

"Believe me, no one could've been more surprised than I was," Art replied. He looked past them and snapped his fingers at Alexei. "But go on, Sirens... give us another story. What else is going on, out in that mad, wonderful world?"

Alexei reviewed the paper with a crinkle. "Well, as you're clearly disposed for more good news: I may report there is talk at the Board of Financiers of a tax refund this year. Rumor has it, we are all in for a rather substantial check in the next month or two."

Horus cleared his throat. "Well now, *I* may know something about that."

Alexei looked at him wide-eyed. "Really? Well, don't hold out, Mr. Templar! Is it going to be the big kick-back they say?"

"Let's put it this way, Captain," Horus began delicately. "I wouldn't go out and make any major purchases ahead of time, if I were you."

"Oh poo," Alexei lamented, folding the paper up. "I suppose it was too good to be true."

"Yes. But enough current events. We should be making history, rather than reading it. My client's still waiting."

The latch on the cell door came unbolted with a jingling twist of Alexei's key ring. "There we are, now," Alexei said, opening the cell. "Free and clear at last."

Horus grinned in on his client. "You heard the man, Rythigaar. You have a long journey ahead of you, and it starts now. I hope you're all packed."

Rythigaar stood. "I'm as fit to travel as may be." He patted the vest of his uniform as if to check it. "I'm already wearing all my earthly possessions."

"That'll have to do," Horus said, waving him out. "I've already arranged for everything else you'll need."

"*Someone* did, anyway," Mallard quipped.

As Rythigaar was passing the door, Alexei removed his police bobby. "Excuse me, Sir," he began contritely, "but I don't believe I ever formally apologized for shooting you. I am very sorry for that."

"It is more than alright, Officer," Rythigaar absolved him. "If you hadn't shot me, I don't know where I'd be now."

Alexei eyed him curiously. "From what I understand of the voyage ahead of you, Sir, you don't really know where you're bound to end up, anyway."

"That's true," Rythigaar nodded. "But it's a far better not-knowing."

On the walk back out to the horse-drawn cab, it was Horus and Deborah who lingered behind this time, letting Alexei provide honor guard from the front. As they were coming out of the station, they watched Art practically skip down the stairs...

"How about our little private detective?" Deborah remarked quietly to Horus. "Who would have thought he could turn things around with Blucille? I was so sure he'd blown it. Must be something bigger than both of them at work."

Horus shook his head as they passed Art, who'd stopped to pat the horse on the head – a gesture of goodwill the horse obviously didn't appreciate, coming from a huge canine. "Strange to hear that from you – the one who just the other day was so quick to resist the idea that we're fated."

Deborah shrugged. "Surely *some* things are meant to be. It's just hard to say what they are, until they happen." She paused just before the carriage door, as Horus held it open for her. "Who knows? Maybe I'll be the next to meet someone special."

Horus' leaping gut arrested his pulse. "Wouldn't that be something?" he asked.

She climbed nonchalantly into the cab, at which point Horus reflexively dropped the façade and took up the thousand-yard stare. He didn't know how long he remained that way, still holding the door, when Art finally appeared in front of him...

"You alright, Horus?" he asked. "You look kinda deeply disturbed..."

"Oh, just casting new light on an old resolution again," Horus replied.

* * *

The ride out to the Harbor's edge was a long one... much too long for Horus to brood in such company. Given time and effort, he managed to refocus on the moment at hand, and dismiss present doubts. Anyway, he could tell right off, there'd be plenty of time spent agonizing about it later...

Even by the advanced hour that they finally reached the coast, the mists of the night before still clung stubbornly in vast patches, especially over the waterfront. They could look back and see a colorful sky and a clear day over much of Mt. Norvein, where they'd come from. But the path ahead remained shrouded and unsearchable...

"Here we are," Horus announced, as the last of their feet crunched down onto the sandy beach, the invigorating smell of sunbaked old dead fish meeting their nostrils. They stood just in front of a really nice dinghy, watching it totter on tranquil little waves. "Or, so I assume. Is this really it, Art?"

"Yup," the PI nodded, his cheer a bit diminished. "And wasn't she a beaut?"

Rythigaar approached Art. "I'm forever grateful for the use of your superfluous fishing craft, Mr. Mallard. It is a truly noble sacrifice; I regret that I'm unable to remunerate you."

"Don't mention it, Rythigaar," Art replied, patting him on the shoulder. "That's just me for you... I'm a sacrificey kinda guy. Anyway, I guess a fella can't have everything go right for him, all in one day."

Rythigaar nodded, then turned back to Horus. "Neither could I leave without thanking you again, Mr. Templar. I'll never know what inspired you to work so tirelessly on behalf of a wretched fellow like myself."

"Standing here now, I only wish there was more I could do for you," Horus replied, eyeing Art's boat. "This is quite a lot of boat for one man alone. I was picturing something smaller..."

"And yet how fortunate it was not as you imagined," a voice called from up the coast. "It may be just right for six more."

Horus whirled, and from out of the fog came Primary Administrator Hihvnor. Horus blinked hard to be sure of it... hardly anyone's sudden appearing would have surprised him more. "Hihvnor?" Horus called back. "This is... most unexpected."

"That is well and good, my friend," Hihvnor laughed, sincerely pleased. "Your secretary evidently succeeded in masking our conspiracy to surprise you."

Horus turned to Deborah. "Surprise me?"

She smiled. "Seems that little speech you gave on Imolkyr's behalf inspired some action, Horus. Hihvnor reached out. He wanted me to keep him apprised, if you were able to get Rythigaar out of the slammer. I've been filling him in on all the travel arrangements since."

"Imolkyr?" Horus repeated, scrambling to put it all together. "But does that mean she's...?"

"...Yes, Mr. Templar," Hihvnor interjected, gesturing behind him. "She's *here*. She, and all that remains of her fellows..."

As Horus watched, six spectres in shock-white cloaks also appeared from beyond the veil of the mists. It was about the spookiest thing he'd ever seen... and yet, sublimely triumphant.

"You were right, of course," Hihvnor went on. "In four thousand years, and more, we've not changed their minds. The old arrangement served no one – that was plain. Far better to simply let them go their way."

Horus raised a brow at him. "What if the other Administrators don't agree with how you've handled your prisoners, Hihvnor?"

Hihvnor shrugged. "It has been some centuries since the last time the matter of their captivity was discussed, I am told. I suspect their absence will go unnoticed for a healthy time to come. Perhaps one day, I'll have to make an account of my decision before my fellows. But it is just as likely I won't."

Horus nodded. "I applaud your reasoning. *And* your initiative."

Just then, he watched as Imolkyr walked up to Rythigaar, her steps still noisy as her ancient joints worked against ages of disuse.

"Hello, grandmother," Rythigaar said.

"Hello, grandson," she replied.

Horus felt deeply privileged to witness this, the most moving reunion his eyes had ever beheld. It brought him to the verge of tears.

"This is a chance beyond my wildest hope," Horus admitted as he approached, when he decided it was alright to intrude. "I never thought to see you out in the waking world, Imolkyr."

"Imagine my own surprise," Imolkyr concurred. "Your deeds are truly mighty, Sir Horus Templar. If we should ever reach the Second Universe, we will carry your name thither with great honor."

"Sheer flattery," Horus replied. "A Public Defender should have such luck... to be celebrated in any universe at all."

Imolkyr nodded, and taking notice that the other members of her strike team from antiquity had already set about trying to deduce the boat and its workings, withdrew to assist...

That left Horus and Rythigaar...

"Somehow, a cheerless thought occurs to me, just now," Rythigaar began. "No matter how far we venture... even to the other side of the Undervoid... it will never be far enough to be free from what I did here. It will always be with me."

"Then let it be a reminder," Horus encouraged him. "To always do your best... if not better. You know the darkness that lies behind you. Press on toward the light."

"I will, Horus Templar," he nodded. "I will."

With that, he turned to go, and the Quest for the Gate seemed poised to begin in earnest, without further ado between the seekers and those who would remain behind. But then, after a rather lengthy interval of huddling and muttering by the boat, Rythigaar called back...

"You all must pardon a final, extraneous inquiry. There is one more thing I would ask."

"What is it, Rythigaar?" Horus replied.

"A question for Art Mallard," he explained, gesturing for the boat. "How do you operate this thing?"

"Beats me," Art shrugged. "All I ever did with it was buy it."

* * *

Once they'd all spent a long time sharing suppositions and tiny snippets of half-remembered boat-lore, they at last withdrew to watch as the seven Dark Inquisitors pushed off, fumbling oafishly with the oars. And yet, with the turn of time – slowly, clumsily, but surely – the hapless new sailors made their way out into deeper waters, drifting appropriately north-east. Once their course seemed sure, the solemnity of the moment made a healthy comeback. For most of them it did, anyway. But one was watching the boat a bit more prosaically...

"You know I'll just go out and buy another one," Art said.

Horus ignored him. He just looked on. "It really is an extraordinary thing they do. I grant they're clumsy at it now. But just imagine the mariners they'll be, by the time they reach that distant shore..."

"What a dreamy picture," Deborah joshed him. "Thinking of joining them, Boss?"

He laughed. "Not presently."

"Are you sure?" she asked, concern creeping into her features. "You're getting that distant look in your eye again."

"I'm sure. It's strange, I suppose... how watching someone go so very far away can give you a new appreciation of your own place."

"No doubt you're prepared to tell us all about it," Deborah quipped.

Horus grinned, though his gaze never left the horizon. "I'm thankful to live in a world where people care about what's right. We care enough to fight about it, to hold our ground against time and tide, to endure every kind of captivity... sometimes, even to *die*... whether all at once or a little every day. Oh, we all lose sight of it at times... and some unfortunately never look back. But by and large, I feel like most of us really do the best we can... or, at worst, try to make the best of what we do."

"Naturally," Deborah replied airily. "I mean, can you really envision a different kind of world?"

"I'd rather not try," Horus admitted. "It would be terrible."

"You had that whole speech already made up," Art accused.

"Remind me to show you the rough drafts some time," Horus answered.

They watched quietly a while longer. Getting antsy, Art put his hands in his pockets and kicked a stone over. "For the first time in days, I'm really hungry," he said. "Let's go get some grub."

"One more minute," Horus said, Art's boat really starting to shrink into the distance. "Let's at least see them until they're out of sight."

It didn't even take another minute, and the fog in the bay enveloped the Gate-Seekers...

...And as for what became of them afterwards, there was no way to know...

...And scarcely any way to imagine...

Acknowledgments

In addition to the regular roundup, I'd like to give special thanks to my grandma, who has been an enthusiastic reader and listener, and who thankfully didn't inspire anyone in this book either by schemes of fraud or by spending long years in prison. Thanks, Grandma! A prospective author couldn't hope for a better ear to bend!

I suppose I should also thank Gabrielle-Suzanne Barbot de Villeneuve… though I admit I've never read the actual fairy tale. And while I'm at it, here's a shout-out to Alan Menken, whose creepy piano music kept cycling through my head over and over, the whole time I was trying to write my own version of sneaking around the west wing…

Another special thanks also goes to my mom, for her extraordinarily expedient proof-read. I suppose it's embarrassing for an author to admit I didn't realize that much reading could be done in one day… but oh well! I remain very grateful, as well as amazed!

For More from E.L. Ward…

Visit his personal site, at:

https://www.booksofelward.com

His vast arsenal of backlist titles includes the following:

TITLES IN THE ORPHAN UNIVERSE

HERON PROPHECIES SERIES

The Chocolate Prophecy

HORUS TEMPLAR – PUBLIC DEFENDER SERIES

Horus Templar and the Case of the Wimpy War-Criminal
Horus Templar and the Case of the Iniquitous Inquisitor
Horus Templar and the Case of the Draft-Dodging Drone
Horus Templar and the Case of the Dubious Decedent
Horus Templar and the Case of the Vengeful Vigilant

E.L. Ward is proud to partner with:

MALOB ARTS

MOSTLY A LOT OF BOZOS

Check out his and other creative works at:

www.malobarts.com

Made in the USA
Monee, IL
04 November 2026

67384582R00079